TEACHER'S
Discovery

COPYME
prints

Accents

- *Spanish accents exercise book*
- *Covers 11 rules and*
- *Contains 144 exercises for classroom use*

Written by
José R. Moreno

Managing Editor
Petra Beierling

Page Layout Artist
Rebecca Cober

Series Producer
Petra Beierling

ISBN: 0-7560-0321-0
SKU: B 996

Scope, Purpose & Organization

PURPOSE

A complete compendium of accentuation, this resource book breaks down the language into the 11 rules necessary for mastering the stress in both pronunciation and the written word.

SCOPE AND ORGANIZATION

The book contains 144 easy to reproduce exercises for classroom use. Included are word identification exercises, accentuation of common Spanish names, and tests on all of the rules. Answer sheets are provided in the Answer Key section at the back of the book.

The first section is devoted to words that have a natural stress and do not require a written accent. The second section covers words that require a written accent. Compartmentalizing allows the student to easily commit to memory all 11 rules required to master accentuation for fluency in the Spanish language.

Teacher's Discovery

How To...

TIME

Reading and explaining the rules will take about 10 minutes.
Each exercise in this book will take 10 to 15 minutes to complete.

INSTRUCTIONS

Copy and hand out to the entire class the sheet with the specific rule you want to explain and practice.

Together with all students read the rule and answer all questions your students have. That will take about 10 minutes.

Assign the related exercises as homework for practice and reinforcement.

Table of Contents

TEACHER'S Discovery

Table of Contents (Cont'd)

Table of Contents (Cont'd)

Teacher's Discovery

Table of Contents (Cont'd)

Introduction

Accentuation is learned by studying the stress in word. There are words that have a natural stress and do not require a written accent. When the natural stress is removed from the syllable that contains it and is placed on another syllable, the newly acquired syllable requires a written accent.

In this book, in pages covering **Rules 1 and 2,** there are exercises with words that have a natural stress and do not require a written accent. In pages covering rules **3 through 11,** there are exercises with words that require a written accent.

(Acentuación se aprende estudiando el énfasis en las palabras. Hay palabras que tienen un énfasis natural y no requieren acento escrito. Cuando el énfasis natural es quitado de la sílaba que lo contiene, la nueva sílaba con el énfasis requiere un acento escrito.

En este cuaderno de ejercicios, en las páginas que cubren las **Reglas 1 y 2,** hay ejercicios con palabras que tienen el énfasis natural y no requieren acento escrito. En las páginas que cubren las **Reglas 3 al 11,** hay ejercicios con palabras que requieren un acento escrtito.)

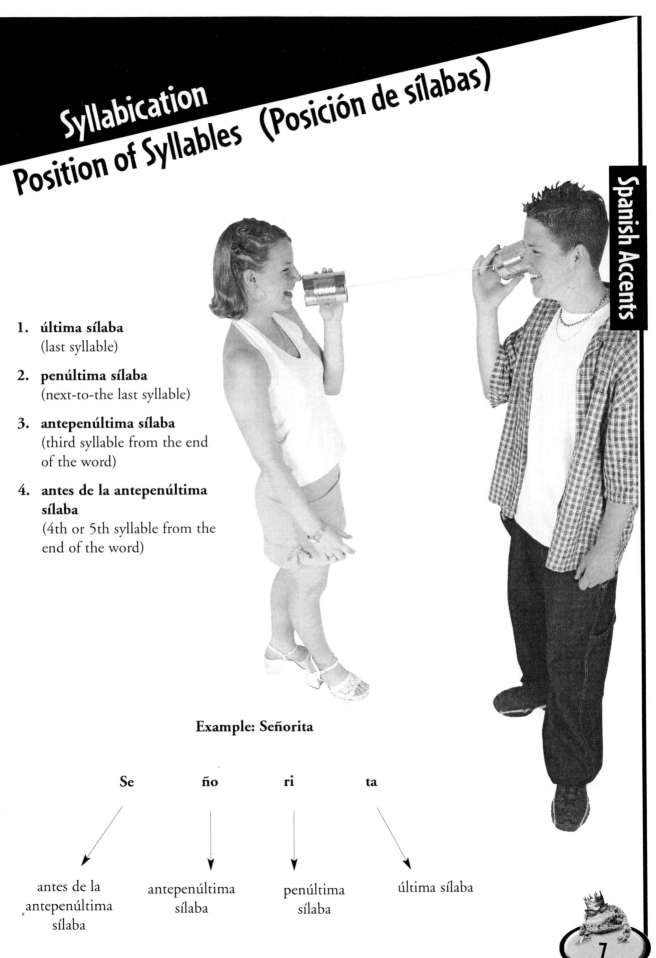

1. **última sílaba**
   (last syllable)

2. **penúltima sílaba**
   (next-to-the last syllable)

3. **antepenúltima sílaba**
   (third syllable from the end
   of the word)

4. **antes de la antepenúltima
   sílaba**
   (4th or 5th syllable from the
   end of the word)

Example: Señorita

Se	ño	ri	ta
↓	↓	↓	↓

antes de la antepenúltima sílaba   antepenúltima sílaba   penúltima sílaba   última sílaba

The Stressed Syllable
The Stress (El Énfasis)

The **stress** can be found in words where the syllable has the highest and strongest sound and in words with a written accent.

(El **énfasis** se puede encontrar en palabras donde la silaba tiene el **sonido más alto** y **más fuerte** y en palabras con **el acento escrito.**)

Examples:

casa	(ca) sa
libertad	li ber (tad)
inglés	in (glés)
lápiz	(lá) piz
médico	(mé) di co

The Accent
(El Acento)

The **written accent** is a small mark that is placed on the vowel of the syllable to indicate the stress.

(El **acento escrito** es una pequeña rayita que se coloca sobre la vocal de la silaba para indicar el énfasis.)

Examples:

1. el   **él**

2. papa   pa **pá**

3. lapiz   **lá** piz

4. japones   ja po **nés**

5. medico   **mé** di co

6. vendeselo   **vén** de se lo

Classification of Words
(Clasificación de Palabras)

In the Spanish Language, words are classified as **four kinds:**

(En el idioma español, las palabras se clasifican en **cuatro clases:**)

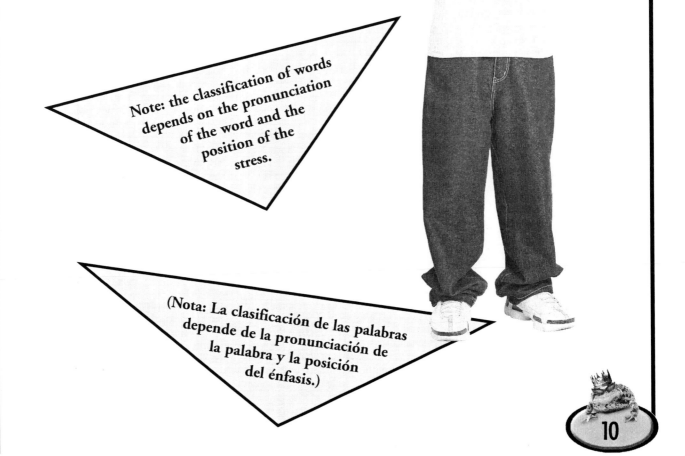

1.   **Agudas**

2.   **Graves**   **(Llanas)**

3.   **Esdrújulas**

4.   **Sobreesdrújulas**

Note: the classification of words depends on the pronunciation of the word and the position of the stress.

(Nota: La clasificación de las palabras depende de la pronunciación de la palabra y la posición del énfasis.)

How do you classify a word as *aguda*, *grave*, *esdrújula*, or *sobreesdrújula*?

(¿Cómo puede clasificar una palabra como **aguda**, **grave**, **esdrújula**, o **sobreesdrújula?**)

Aguda
- is a word that has the stress on the last syllable.
- **(es una palabra que tiene el énfasis en la última silaba.)**

Grave
- is a word that has the stress on the next-to-the-last syllable.
- **(es una palabra que tiene el énfasis en la penúltima sílaba.)**

Esdrújula
- is a word that has the stress on the 3rd syllable from the end of the word.
- **(Es una palabra que tiene el énfasis en la antepenúltima sílaba.)**

Sobreesdrújula
- is a word that has the stress on the 4th or 5th syllable from the end of the word.
- **(es una palabra que tiene el énfasis antes de la antepenúltima sílaba.)**

Classification of Words
Agudas

Words called *agudas* have the stress on the **last syllable.**

(Las palabras llamadas **agudas** tienen el énfasis en la **última sílaba.**)

Examples:

color	co **lor**
administrador	ad mi nis tra **dor**
natural	na tu **ral**
papá	pa **pá**
capitán	ca pi **tán**

(Nota: Algunas palabras agudas tienen un acento escrito.)

Note: Some *Agudas* words have a written accent.

Classification of Words
Graves (Llanas)

Words called *graves* or *llanas* have the stress on the **next-to-the-last syllable.**

(Las palabras llamadas **graves** o **llanas** tienen el énfasis en la **penúltima sílaba.**)

Examples:

casa	**ca** sa
bonita	bo **ni** ta
señorita	se ño **ri** ta
fácil	**fá** cil
azúcar	a **zú** car

Note: some *graves* or *llanas* words have a written accent.

(Nota: Algunas palabras graves o Llanas tienen un acento escrito.)

Esdrújulas

Words called *esdrújulas* have the stress on the **3rd syllable from the end of the word.**

(Las palabras llamadas **esdrújulas** tienen el énfasis en la **antepenúltima sílaba.**)

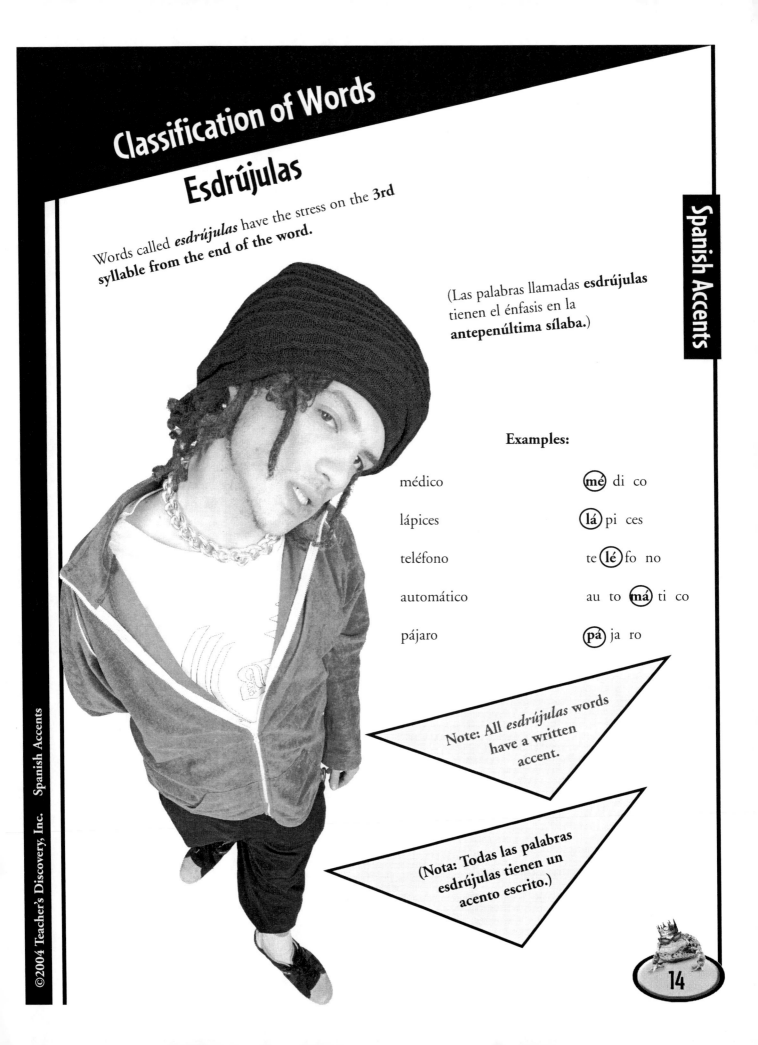

Examples:

médico	**mé** di co
lápices	**lá** pi ces
teléfono	te **lé** fo no
automático	au to **má** ti co
pájaro	**pá** ja ro

Note: All *esdrújulas* words have a written accent.

(Nota: Todas las palabras esdrújulas tienen un acento escrito.)

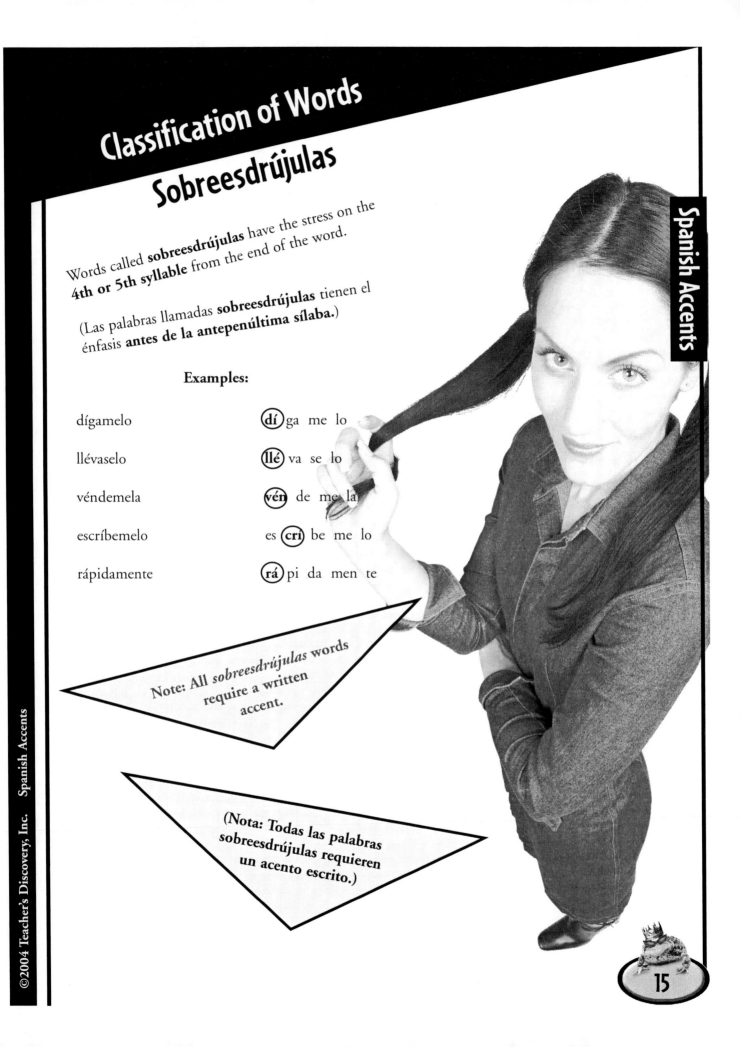

Classification of Words
Sobreesdrújulas

Words called **sobreesdrújulas** have the stress on the **4th or 5th syllable** from the end of the word.

(Las palabras llamadas **sobreesdrújulas** tienen el énfasis **antes de la antepenúltima sílaba.**)

Examples:

dígamelo	**dí** ga me lo
llévaselo	**llé** va se lo
véndemela	**vén** de me la
escríbemelo	es **cri** be me lo
rápidamente	**rá** pi da men te

Note: All *sobreesdrújulas* words require a written accent.

(Nota: Todas las palabras sobreesdrújulas requieren un acento escrito.)

Important information
(Información importante)

1. **Capital letters** that require a written accent should be accented.
   (**Las letras mayúsculas** que requieren un acento escrito se deben acentuar.)

   | **Examples:** | Oscar, África | (see p. 100) |

2. **Monosyllable words** are one syllable words. These words are called **agudas**.
   (**Las palabras monosílabas** son de una sílaba. Estas palabras se llaman **agudas**.)

   | **Examples:** | el, se, de, tú | (see p. 142) |

3. **Diacritic words** are spelled the same but one has an accent to distinguish another function.
   (**Las palabras diacríticas** se escriben igual pero una tiene el acento escrito para distinguir otra función.)

   | **Examples:** | el, él, tu, tú | (see p. 142) |

4. **Adverbs** that combine with the suffix "mente" have two stresses. The adverb maintains the written accent.
   (**Los adverbios** que combinan con el sufijo "mente" tienen dos énfasis. El adverbio mantiene el acento escrito.)

   | **Examples:** | rápidamente, fácilmente | (see p. 168) |

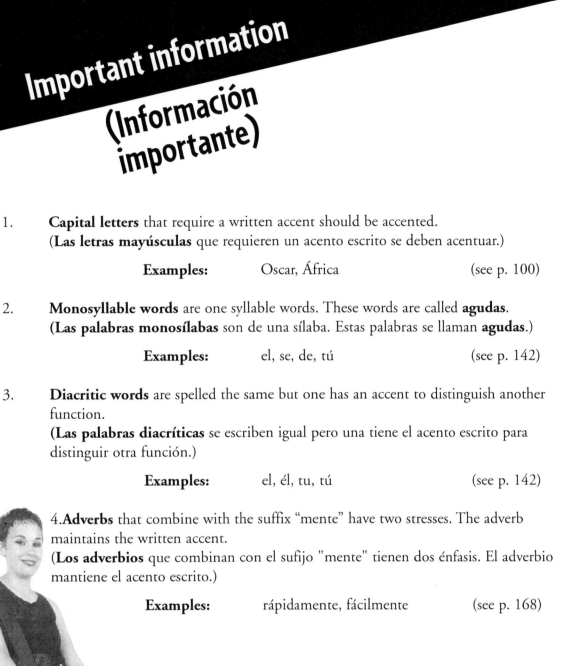

Accent Rules

Rules: 1 & 2
Require no written accent!

Rules: 3 through 11
Require a written accent!

Accents
Rule 1

Words that end in a vowel (a, e, i, o, u), *n* or *s*, stress regularly on the next-to-the-last syllable and do not require a written accent.

Palabras que terminan con una vocal (a, e, i, o, u), o con las consonantes *n* o *s* normalmente tienen el énfasis en la penúltima sílaba y no requieren acento escrito.

Examples:
1. casa   (ca) sa   (house)
2. mano   (ma) no   (hand)
3. bonito   bo (ni) to   (pretty)
4. señoritas   se ño (ri) tas   (ladies)
5. americano   a me ri (ca) no   (american)

These words are called *graves* or *llanas*.

Exercise

This exercise has words that contain only two syllables.

(Este ejercicio tiene palabras que contienen dos sílabas.)

These words do not require a written accent.

(Estas palabras no requieren acento escrito.)

These words are called *Graves*

Divide the words into syllables and circle the syllable stressed.
(Divida las palabras en sílabas y rodee la sílaba que tenga el énfasis.)

1. mesa   _____ (table)
2. hijo   _____ (son)
3. gato   _____ (cat)
4. rojo   _____ (red)
5. niño   _____ (boy)
6. nota   _____ (note)
7. malo   _____ (bad)
8. hija   _____ (daughter)
9. toro   _____ (bull)
10. rico   _____ (rich)
11. alto   _____ (tall)
12. sala   _____ (living room)
13. boca   _____ (mouth)
14. luna   _____ (moon)
15. baño   _____ (bath)

Accents Exercise

This exercise has two syllable words that have NO accent.

(Este ejercicio tiene palabras de dos sílabas que NO requieren acento escrito.)

Name: _____

Date: _____

Class: _____

These words end in a vowel, *n* or *s*, and stress the next-to-the-last syllable.

(Estas palabras terminan en una vocal, *n* o *s*, y tienen el énfasis en la penúltima sílaba.)

These words are called *graves*

Divide the words into syllables and circle the syllable stressed.
(Divida las palabras en sílabas y rodee la sílaba que tenga el énfasis.)

1. calle   (ca)lle _____ (street)
2. perro   _____ (dog)
3. silla   _____ (chair)
4. leche   _____ (milk)
5. padre   _____ (father)
6. libro   _____ (book)
7. mucho   _____ (a lot)
8. lunes   _____ (Monday)
9. joven   _____ (young)
10. carta   _____ (letter)
11. plumas   _____ (pens)
12. dulce   _____ (candy)
13. flores   _____ (flowers)
14. nuevo   _____ (new)
15. tienda   _____ (store)

Exercise
Popular Names

The following popular names are *graves* words. They contain two syllables only.

(Los siguientes nombres populares son palabras graves. Estas palabras contienen dos sílabas.)

Divide the names into syllables and circle the syllable stressed.
(Divada los nombres en sílabas y rodee la sílaba que tenga el énfasis.)

1. Ana   (A) na _____

2. Rosa _____

3. Rita _____

4. Edna _____

5. Olga _____

6. Dora _____

7. Carlos _____

8. Mario _____

9. Pedro _____

10. Diana _____

11. Pablo _____

12. Irma _____

13. Julio _____

14. Blanca _____

15. Carmen _____

Grave Words

Write the following *graves* words and
circle the syllable stressed.

(Escriba las palabras graves y rodee la
sílaba con el énfasis.)

Name: _____

Date: _____

Class: _____

Divide the words, circle the stressed syllable.
(Divida las palabras, rodee la sílaba con el énfasis.

1. dulces _____
2. rojo _____
3. libro _____
4. tienda _____
5. joven _____
6. lunes _____
7. mesa _____
8. carta _____
9. Pedro _____
10. calle _____
11. alto _____
12. Carmen _____
13. muchos _____
14. Ana _____
15. nuevos _____
16. sala _____
17. leche _____
18. Diana _____
19. toro _____
20. Mario _____

Sentence Exercise

Write the sentences; circle the stress on all
two syllable words.

(Escriba las oraciones, rodee la sílaba con el
énfasis en las palabras de dos sílabas.)

Name: _____

Date: _____

Class: _____

1	Dora y Pedro hablan con el joven.

2	Julio es hijo de Blanca.

3	La tienda nueva vende pan, leche y dulces.

4	A mi padre le gusta el libro de Carmen.

5	En la casa tengo una mesa con cinco sillas.

6	El gato negro de Mario es malo.

7	Rita y Pablo tienen un carro rojo.

8	El toro grande corre mucho.

9	Irma tiene muchas flores en la sala.

10	La hija de Edna es alta y joven.

Paragraph Using Graves Words

Name: _____

Date: _____

Class: _____

This paragraph contains *graves* words only and do not require a written accent.

(Este párrafo contiene palabras graves nada más y no requieren acento escrito.)

Read the paragraph; circle the stressed syllable on words with two syllables.

(Lea el párrafo, rodee la sílaba con el énfasis en palabras de dos sílabas.)

Yo soy padre de tres hijos. Todos son ricos. Mi hijo se llama Carlos. Es un joven bueno y muy alto que vive en una casa chica. Su niño tiene un perro muy grande y un gato muy malo. Mis hijas se llaman Olga y Diana. Ellas tienen una casa nueva y en la sala tienen una mesa roja con muchas sillas. Ellas viven cerca de mi casa. Diana tiene un carro nuevo. Siempre vienen a mi casa los lunes.

Exercise

Name: _____

Date: _____

Class: _____

Graves words always stress on the next-to-the-last syllable, even if the word has three or more syllables.

(Las palabras graves siempre tienen el énfasis en la penúltima sílaba, aunque la palabra tenga tres sílabas o más.)

These words are called *graves*.

1 Rule 1

When you pronounce the words, the syllable stressed is found by having the highest sound.

(Cuando pronuncie las palabras, la sílaba que tiene el énfasis se nota por el sonido más alto.)

Divide the words, circle the stressed syllable.
Divida las palabras, rodee la sílaba con el énfasis.

1.	bonita	bo (ni) ta _____	(pretty)
2.	mañana	_____	(tomorrow)
3.	dinero	_____	(money)
4.	amigo	_____	(friend)
5.	zapato	_____	(shoe)
6.	pizarra	_____	(board)
7.	pelota	_____	(ball)
8.	hermano	_____	(brother)
9.	comida	_____	(food)
10.	familia	_____	(family)
11.	papeles	_____	(papers)
12.	hermosa	_____	(beautiful)

25

Exercise

All these words end in a vowel (a, e, i, o, u) or the consonants *n* or *s*.

(Todas estas palabras terminan en una vocal (a, e, i, o, u) o con las consonantes *n* o *s*.)

These words are called *graves*.

Name: _____

Date: _____

Class: _____

These *Graves* words of four and five syllables still have the stress on the next-to-the-last syllable and require no written accent.

(Estas palabras graves de cuatro o cinco silabas, también tienen el énfasis en la penúltima sílaba y no requieren acento escrito.)

Read the words, divide into syllables and circle the stressed syllable.
(Lea las palabras, divida en sílabas y rodee la sílaba que tenga el énfasis.)

1. señorita   se ño (ri) ta _____ (young lady)
2. carretera   _____ (highway)
3. escritorio   _____ (desk)
4. presidente   _____ (president)
5. chocolate   _____ (chocolate)
6. mexicano   _____ (mexican)
7. secretaria   _____ (secretary)
8. americano   _____ (american)
9. apartamento   _____ (apartment)
10. inteligente   _____ (intelligent)

Exercise
Spanish Popular Names

Name: _____

Date: _____

Class: _____

The following popular names are *Graves* words. They contain three, four, and five syllables.

(Los siguientes nombres populares son palabras graves.
Estas palabras contienen tres, cuatro y cinco sílabas.

Divide the names into syllables and circle the stressed syllable.

(Divida los nombres en sílabas y rodee la sílaba que tenga el énfasis.)

1.   Roberto   Ro (ber) to _____
2.   Felipe   _____
3.   Ricardo   _____
4.   Eduardo   _____
5.   Antonio   _____
6.   Patricia   _____
7.   Leticia   _____
8.   Graciela   _____
9.   Armando   _____
10. Esteban   _____
11. Francisco   _____
12. Josefina   _____
13. Guadalupe   _____
14. Evangelina   _____
15. Maximiliano   _____

Exercise
Graves Words

Name: _____

Date: _____

Class: _____

Write the following *graves* words and circle the stressed syllable.

(Escriba las siguientes palabras graves y rodee la sílaba con el énfasis.)

1. secretarias _____
2. plumas _____
3. familia _____
4. calle _____
5. Diana _____
6. pizarra _____
7. apartamento _____
8. hermosa _____
9. niño _____
10. americano _____
11. perros _____
12. tiendas _____
13. papeles _____
14. presidente _____
15. bonitas _____
16. mucha _____
17. escritorios _____
18. carta _____
19. carretera _____
20. amigo _____

Sentence Exercise

Write the sentences; circle the stress on all two or more syllable words.

(Escriba las frases, rodee el énfasis en las palabras de dos o más sílabas.)

Name: _____

Date: _____

Class: _____

1 Rule 1

1	Mi amigo tiene mucho dinero.
2	Eduardo compra comida y flores.
3	El presidente vive con su familia.
4	La secretaria vende los chocolates mexicanos.
5	Mario estudia en su escritorio.
6	Mi hermano es joven y alto.
7	Josefina habla mucho con Patricia.
8	Mi padre tiene una tienda de zapatos.
9	El muchacho corre por la calle.
10	Pedro bebe mucha leche.

Paragraph Using Graves Words

Name: _____

Date: _____

Class: _____

This paragraph contains *graves* words only and do not require a written accent.

(Este párrafo contiene palabras graves nada más y no requieren acento escrito.)

Read the paragraph; circle the stressed syllable on words with two or more syllables.

(Lea el párrafo, rodee la sílaba con el énfasis en palabras de dos o más sílabas.)

Mi padre Francisco tiene un hermano que tiene una tienda de comida. Su nombre es Ricardo y es el presidente de su negocio. Ricardo es muy inteligente y vive en un apartamento grande con su familia. Su esposa Guadalupe es muy bonita y es su secretaria. Sus hijas Diana y Patricia son estudiantes y asisten al colegio. Ellas estudian para ser profesoras y en las noches trabajan en la tienda.

Test

Read the *graves* words, divide into syllables, and circle the stressed syllable.

(Lea las palabras graves, divida en sílabas y rodee la sílaba con el énfasis.)

Name: _____

Date: _____

Class: _____

1. mexicano _____
2. pelota _____
3. muchos _____
4. Carmen _____
5. hermano _____
6. libro _____
7. dinero _____
8. nuevo _____
9. bonito _____
10. Evangelina _____
11. zapatos _____
12. leche _____
13. Pedro _____
14. inteligente _____
15. mañana _____
16. señorita _____
17. silla _____
18. chocolate _____
19. Guadalupe _____
20. flores _____

Information

The next Rule (#2) contains exercises that include words that do not require a written accent covered in rule #1.

Rules #3 through #11 contain exercises that include words that have written accents.

(La siguiente regla (#2) contiene ejercicios que incluyen palabras que no requieren un acento escrito cubiertas en la regla #1.

Las reglas #3 al #11 contienen ejercicios que contienen palabras que tienen acentos escritos.)

2 | Rule 2

©2004 Teacher's Discovery, Inc.   Spanish Accents

Accents
Rule 2

Words that end in a consonant, except *n* or *s*, with a stress on the last syllable require NO written accent.

Las palabras que terminan con una consonante, excepto *n* o *s* tienen el énfasis en la última sílaba y NO requieren acento.

These words are called *agudas*

Examples:

1. color	co lor	(color)
2. azul	a zul	(blue)
3. hospital	hos pi tal	(hospital)
4. felicidad	fe li ci dad	(happiness)
5. universidad	u ni ver si dad	(university)

Exercise

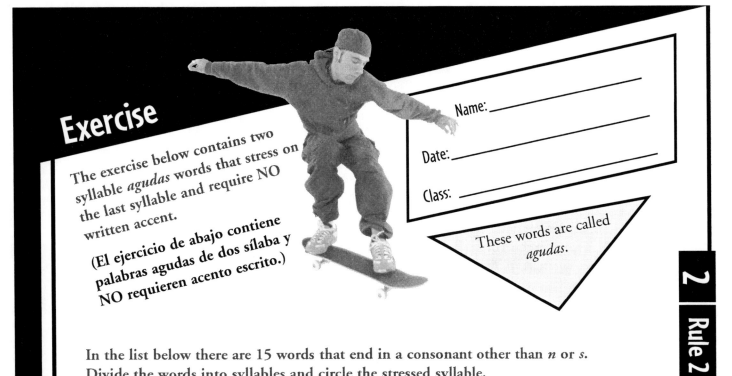

The exercise below contains two syllable *agudas* words that stress on the last syllable and require NO written accent.

(El ejercicio de abajo contiene palabras agudas de dos sílaba y NO requieren acento escrito.)

Name: _____

Date: _____

Class: _____

These words are called *agudas*.

In the list below there are 15 words that end in a consonant other than *n* or *s*. Divide the words into syllables and circle the stressed syllable.

(En la lista de abajo hay 15 palabras que terminan en una consonante excepto *n* o *s*. Divida en sílabas y rodee el énfasis.)

1.	papel	pa (pel) _____	(paper)
2.	mujer	_____	(woman)
3.	plural	_____	(plural)
4.	feliz	_____	(happy)
5.	ciudad	_____	(city)
6.	hotel	_____	(hotel)
7.	ayer	_____	(yesterday)
8.	reloj	_____	(watch)
9.	local	_____	(local)
10.	motor	_____	(motor)
11.	central	_____	(central)
12.	salud	_____	(health)
13.	doctor	_____	(doctor)
14.	señor	_____	(man)
15.	nariz	_____	(nose)

Exercise
Spanish Names (Agudas)

The following Spanish names are *AGUDAS* WORDS that contain two syllables and require NO written accent.

(Los siguientes nombres en español son PALABRAS AGUDAS que tienen dos sílabas y NO requieren un acento escrito.)

2 | Rule 2

Divide the names into syllables and circle the stressed syllable.
(Divida los nombres en sílabas y rodee la sílaba que tenga el énfasis.)

1. Abel   A (bel) _____
2. Eloy   _____
3. Fidel   _____
4. Omar   _____
5. Ines   _____
6. David   _____
7. Vidal   _____
8. Feliz   _____
9. Daniel   _____
10. Raquel   _____
11. Gabriel   _____
12. Manuel   _____
13. Ortiz   _____
14. Samuel   _____
15. Miguel   _____

Exercise
Agudas and GravesWords

Name: _____

Date: _____

Class: _____

Write the following words and circle the stressed syllable.

(Escriba las palabras y rodee la sílaba con el énfasis.)

2 | Rule 2

1. usted   _____
2. lunes   _____
3. hablan   _____
4. doctor   _____
5. Julio   _____
6. arroz   _____
7. David   _____
8. joven   _____
9. plural   _____
10. hijos   _____
11. ciudad   _____
12. mujer   _____
13. salud   _____
14. dulce   _____
15. Fidel   _____
16. reloj   _____
17. comen   _____
18. ayer   _____
19. azul   _____
20. amen   _____

ccents

36

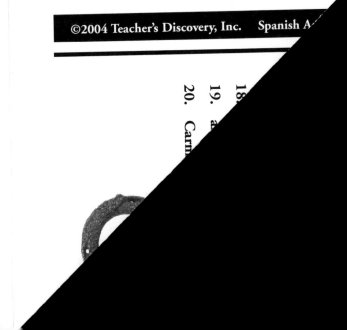

18
19. a
20. Carn

Sentence Exercise

Write the sentences; circle the stress on all two or more syllable words.

(Escriba las oraciones, rodee el énfasis en las palabras de dos o más sílabas.)

Name: _____

Date: _____

Class: _____

1 Felix habla con el joven en el hotel.

2 Ayer Patricia y Raquel hablaban con el doctor.

3 El carro de Daniel es color azul.

4 En esa tienda se venden papel y plumas.

5 En la ciudad de San Antonio vive Manuel Ortiz.

6 El reloj nuevo de Miguel se vende por mucho dinero.

7 Esa mujer alta se llama Ines Barrientos.

8 La camioneta de Vidal tiene un motor grande.

9 La oficina central tiene un departamento de salud.

10 El amigo de Gabriel tiene la nariz quebrada.

Exercise
Word Identification

Identify all words as agudas or graves.
(Identifique las palabras como agudas o graves.)

A-Aguda	G-Grave

1. joven _____
2. nariz _____
3. ciudad _____
4. hermanos _____
5. Esteban _____
6. ayer _____
7. Carmen _____
8. mujer _____
9. plural _____
10. flores _____
11. Patricia _____
12. salud _____
13. hotel _____
14. familias _____
15. Marisol _____
16. secretaria _____
17. dulces _____
18. feliz _____
19. Armando _____
20. reloj _____

Paragraph with Agudas and Graves Words

This paragraph contains *agudas* and *graves* words and do not require a written accent.

(Este párrafo contiene palabras agudas y graves y no requieren acento escrito.)

Read the paragraph; circle the stressed syllable on all *agudas* and *graves* words.

(Lea el párrafo, rodee la sílaba con el énfasis en las palabras agudas y graves.)

2 | Rule 2

Francisco habla con Miguel en su
apartamento. Quiere comprar un carro azul.
Ayer hablaba con el dueño del carro. Se llama
Daniel Ortiz y vive en la ciudad de Laredo.
Es doctor y tiene su oficina en un hotel cerca
de la carretera. Mi secretaria Raquel lo
conoce. Dice que vive muy feliz con su mujer
y con sus dos hijos Abel y Omar. Tienen el
carro en un local de venta.

Test

Write the words, divide into syllables, and circle the stressed syllable, and identify as *agudas* or *graves*.

(Escriba las palabras, divida en sílabas y rodee la sílaba con el énfasis e identifique como agudas o graves.)

A or G

1. altos
2. Gabriel
3. pizarra
4. doctor
5. presidente
6. azul
7. señor
8. David
9. calles
10. pluma
11. nariz
12. Ricardo
13. Sandoval
14. padre
15. mujer
16. Graciela
17. americano
18. ciudad
19. Ortiz
20. tienda

Exercise

Agudas words always stress on the last syllable, even if the word has three or more syllables.

(Las palabras agudas siempre tienen el énfasis en la última sílaba, aunque la palabra tenga tres sílabas o más.)

The following words end in a consonant, except *n* or *s*, and require NO written accent.

(Las siguientes palabras terminan en una consonante, excepto *n* o *s* y NO requieren acento escrito.)

2 | Rule 2

These words are called *agudas*

Divide into syllables, and circle the stressed syllable.
(Divida en sílabas y rodee la sílaba que tenga el énfasis.)

1. general   ge ne (ral) _____ (general)
2. regular   _____ (regular)
3. Navidad   _____ (Christmas)
4. singular   _____ (singular)
5. español   _____ (Spanish)
6. profesor   _____ (teacher)
7. capital   _____ (capital)
8. libertad   _____ (liberty)
9. superior   _____ (superior)
10. nacional   _____ (national)
11. amistad   _____ (friendship)
12. director   _____ (director)

Exercise

The following *AGUDAS* words have four or five syllables and require NO written accent.

(Las siguientes palabras AGUDAS tienen cuatro o cinco sílabas y NO requieren acento escrito.)

These words are called *agudas*

2 | Rule 2

Divide into syllables and circle the stressed syllable.
(Divida en sílabas y rodee la sílaba que tenga el énfasis.)

1. calculador   cal cu la (dor) _____
2. residencial _____
3. ferrocarril _____
4. televisor _____
5. dificultad _____
6. humanidad _____
7. felicidad _____
8. enfermedad _____
9. universidad _____
10. administrador _____
11. investigador _____
12. personalidad _____

42

Exercise
Spanish Names (Agudas)

The following Spanish names are *agudas* words that have two, three, and four syllables and require NO written accent.

(Los siguientes nombres en español son palabras agudas que tienen dos, tres y cuatro sílabas y NO requieren un acento escrito.)

Name: _____

Date: _____

Class: _____

2 Rule 2

Divide the words, circle the stressed syllable.
(**Divida las palabras, rodee la sílaba con el énfasis**).

1. Javier   Ja (vier) _____
2. Isabel   _____
3. Rafael   _____
4. Israel   _____
5. Amador   _____
6. Escobar   _____
7. Salvador   _____
8. Marisol   _____
9. Ismael   _____
10. Aguilar   _____
11. Sandoval   _____
12. Esquivel   _____
13. Veracruz   _____
14. Apolinar   _____
15. Villarreal _____

Exercise

Agudas and Graves Words

Divide the following words and circle the stressed syllable.

(Divida las siguientes palabras y rodee la sílaba con el énfasis.)

Name: _____

Date: _____

Class: _____

1. amistad _____
2. papeles _____
3. nariz _____
4. regular _____
5. presidente _____
6. dificultad _____
7. doctores _____
8. Esquivel _____
9. calles _____
10. hospital _____
11. investigador _____
12. nacional _____
13. Veracruz _____
14. señoritas _____
15. felicidad _____
16. muchos _____
17. ferrocarril _____
18. Aguilar _____
19. zapatos _____
20. Eduardo _____

Sentence Exercise

Write the sentences; circle the stressed syllable
on all *agudas* and *graves* words.

Escriba las oraciones, rodee la sílaba con el
énfasis en todas las palabras agudas y graves.)

2 | Rule 2

1	El administrador es hermano de Manuel Villarreal.
2	Mi padre escribe cartas en español.
3	El director del centro de salud es Javier.
4	Carlos y Amador tienen muy buena amistad.
5	Israel es profesor en la universidad.
6	El señor Ricardo sufre de una enfermedad mala.
7	El ferrocarril pasa por la capital nacional.
8	El joven es muy feliz con su novia.
9	El presidente tiene una personalidad muy bonita.
10	La señorita Diana trabaja en el hospital general.

45

Exercise
Word Identification

Identify all words as agudas or graves.
(Identifique las palabras como agudas o graves.)

Name: _____

Date: _____

Class: _____

A-Aguda	G-Grave

1. superior _____
2. hablaban _____
3. señoritas _____
4. residencial _____
5. plumas _____
6. Salvador _____
7. libertad _____
8. chocolates _____
9. Graciela _____
10. natural _____
11. calculador _____
12. reloj _____
13. inteligentes _____
14. Navidad _____
15. Carmen _____
16. singular _____
17. Marisol _____
18. pizarra _____
19. joven _____
20. humanidad _____

Exercise

Paragraphs with Agudas and Graves Words

Name: _____

Date: _____

Class: _____

These paragraphs contain *agudas* and *graves* words and do not require a written accent.

(Estos *párrafos* contienen palabras agudas y graves y no requieren acento escrito.)

Read the paragraphs, circle the stressed syllable on all *agudas* and *graves* words.

(Lea los *párrafos*, rodee la *sílaba* con el *énfasis* en las palabras agudas y graves.)

2 | Rule 2

El padre de Marisol se llama Pedro Escobar. Trabaja en la ciudad de El Paso en el Departamento de Salud. Tiene muy buena amistad con el doctor porque habla español muy bien.

La secretaria del administrador de la universidad se llama Olga Sandoval. Ella es una mujer muy inteligente pero tiene dificultad con el español. Ayer ella hablaba con el profesor Aguilar.

Test

Write the words, divide into syllables, and circle the stressed syllable, and identify as *agudas* or *graves*.

(Escriba las palabras, divida en sílabas, rodee la sílaba con el énfasis e identifique como agudas o graves.)

Name: _____

Date: _____

Class: _____

A or G

1. mexicano _____

2. libertad _____

3. amigos _____

4. Francisco _____

5. reloj _____

6. nacional _____

7. feliz _____

8. comida _____

9. Isabel _____

10. joven _____

11. residencial _____

12. ayer _____

13. Diana _____

14. escritorios _____

15. amistad _____

16. carreteras _____

17. rojo _____

18. personalidad _____

19. Manuel _____

20. Carmen _____

Accents
Rule 3

Words that end in a vowel (a, e, i, o, u), *n* or *s*, with a stress on the last syllable require a written accent.

Las palabras que terminan con una vocal (a, e, i, o, u), *n* o *s*, con el énfasis en la última sílaba requieren acento escrito.

These words are called *agudas*

Examples:
1. mamá
2. inglés
3. capitán
4. autobús
5. estudiaré

ma **má**
in **glés**
ca pi **tán**
au to **bús**
es tu dia **ré**

(mother)
(English)
(captain)
(bus)
(will study)

Exercise

Name: _____

Date: _____

Class: _____

Agudas words end in a vowel (a, e, i, o, u), *n* or s, stress the last syllable and require a written accent.

(Palabras agudas que terminan con una vocal (a,e,i,o,u), *n* o *s*, y tienen el énfasis en la última sílaba, requieren un acento escrito.)

These words are called *agudas*

In the following exercises, you will work with *Agudas* words of two or more syllables that require a written accent.

(En los siguientes ejercicios, trabajarás con palabras agudas de dos sílabas o más que requieren un acento escrito.)

Divide into syllables, circle the stressed syllable and apply the accent.
(Divida en sílabas, rodee la sílaba que tenga el énfasis y aplique el acento.)

1. papa   pa (pá) _____   (father)
2. violin   _____   (violin)
3. adios   _____   (goodbye)
4. millon   _____   (million)
5. aqui   _____   (here)
6. jardin   _____   (garden)
7. sofa   _____   (sofa)
8. frances   _____   (French)
9. alli   _____   (there)
10. despues   _____   (after)
11. tambien   _____   (also)
12. cafe   _____   (coffee)

Exercise

The following *agudas* words are verbs that end in a vowel (a, e, i, o, u), *n* or *s*, stress the last syllable and require a written accent.

(Las siguientes palabras agudas son verbos que terminan con una vocal (a,e,i,o,u) *n* o *s*, tienen el énfasis en la última sílaba y requieren un acento escrito.)

These words are called *agudas*

These *agudas* words are verbs used in the preterit and future tenses.

(Estas palabras agudas son verbos que se usan en los tiempos pretérito y futuro.)

3 | Rule 3

Divide into syllables, circle the stressed syllable and apply the accent.
(Divida en sílabas, rodee la sílaba que tenga el énfasis y aplique el acento.

1.	hable	ha (blé) _____	(I talked)
2.	comi	_____	(I ate)
3.	vivio	_____	(He lived)
4.	abri	_____	(I opened)
5.	vendio	_____	(He sold)
6.	bebi	_____	(I drank)
7.	compro	_____	(He bought)
8.	ire	_____	(I will go)
9.	veras	_____	(You will see)
10.	seran	_____	(They will be)
11.	entre	_____	(I entered)
12.	dare	_____	(I shall give)

Exercise
Spanish Names (Agudas)

The following Spanish names are *agudas* words that have two syllables and require a written accent.

(Los siguientes nombres en español son palabras agudas que tienen dos sílabas y requieren un acento escrito.)

Name: _____

Date: _____

Class: _____

Divide the names into syllables, circle the stressed syllable and apply the accent.

(Divida los nombres en sílabas, rodee la sílaba que tenga el énfasis y aplique el acento.)

1. Jose   Jo (sé) _____
2. Martin _____
3. Jesus _____
4. Ruben _____
5. Ramon _____
6. Tomas _____
7. Andres _____
8. Rene _____
9. Adrian _____
10. Cantu _____
11. Ines _____
12. Galvan _____
13. Solis _____
14. Chacon _____
5. Roman _____

52

Accents Exercise

Write the following words, circle the stressed syllable, and add the accent if necessary.

(Escriba las palabras, rodee la sílaba con el énfasis y aplique el acento si es necesario.)

Name: _____

Date: _____

Class: _____

1. dulces _____
2. frances _____
3. ciudad _____
4. aqui _____
5. flores _____
6. felicidad _____
7. Isabel _____
8. adios _____
9. Solis _____
10. feliz _____
11. Carmen _____
12. tambien _____
13. central _____
14. despues _____
15. violin _____
16. ire _____
17. padre _____
18. profesor _____
19. jardin _____
20. Esteban _____

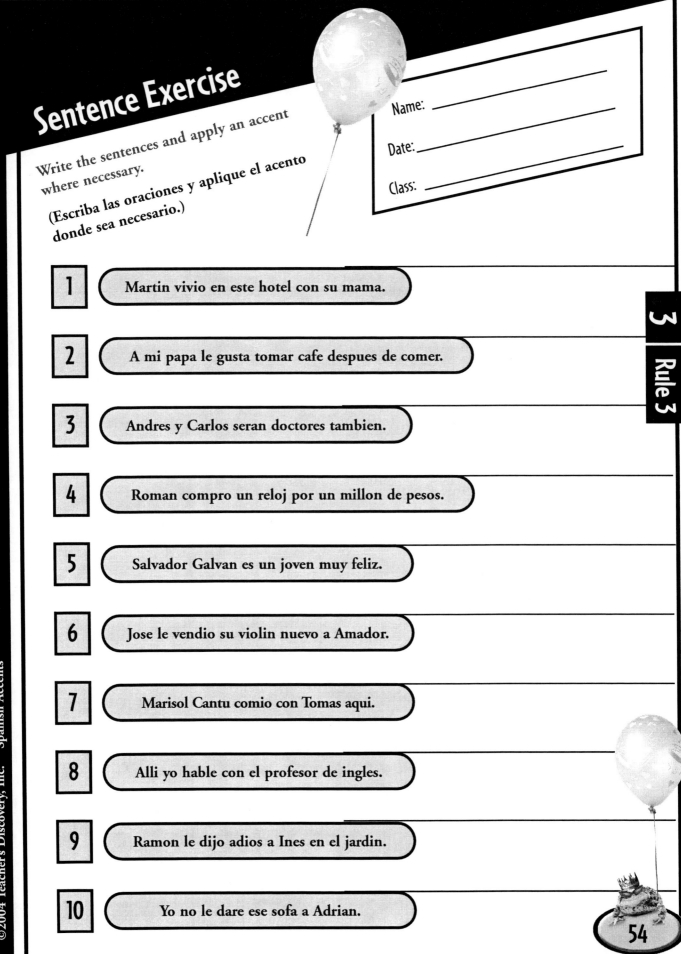

Sentence Exercise

Write the sentences and apply an accent where necessary.

(Escriba las oraciones y aplique el acento donde sea necesario.)

Name: _____

Date: _____

Class: _____

1 Martin vivio en este hotel con su mama.

2 A mi papa le gusta tomar cafe despues de comer.

3 Andres y Carlos seran doctores tambien.

4 Roman compro un reloj por un millon de pesos.

5 Salvador Galvan es un joven muy feliz.

6 Jose le vendio su violin nuevo a Amador.

7 Marisol Cantu comio con Tomas aqui.

8 Alli yo hable con el profesor de ingles.

9 Ramon le dijo adios a Ines en el jardin.

10 Yo no le dare ese sofa a Adrian.

Exercise
Word Identification

Add accents if necessary and identify all words as *agudas* or *graves*.

(Escriba los acentos si es necesario e identifique las palabras como agudas o graves.)

Name: _____

Date: _____

Class: _____

3 | **Rule 3**

	A-Aguda	G-Grave
1.	tiendas	_____
2.	vendio	_____
3.	Jesus	_____
4.	Apolinar	_____
5.	Mario	_____
6.	despues	_____
7.	humanidad	_____
8.	familia	_____
9.	feliz	_____
10.	lunes	_____
11.	Chacon	_____
12.	Antonio	_____
13.	adios	_____
14.	Esquivel	_____
15.	universidad	_____
16.	vivio	_____
17.	singular	_____
18.	hablan	_____
19.	tambien	_____
20.	reloj	_____

Exercise
Paragraphs with Accents

These paragraphs contain words that do require a written accent.

(Estos párrafos contienen palabras que requieren un acento escrito.)

Name: _____

Date: _____

Class: _____

Read the paragraphs and apply accent if necessary.

(Lea los párrafos y aplique acentos si son necesarios.)

La mama de Ruben se llama Blanca. Ella vivio en San Antonio con su hermano Rene. Alli ella hablo puro ingles y nada de español. Yo tambien ire a esa ciudad, pero yo quiero aprender frances.

Jose vendio su carro. Hace dos años lo compro por un millon de pesos. Mi papa insiste que compre la camioneta de Tomas y que tambien compre el violin de Ramon. Mañana ire con ellos a comprar las dos cosas.

Test

Write the words, add the accent if necessary, and identify as *agudas* or *graves*

Escriba las palabras, aplique el acento si es necesario e identifique como agudas o graves.)

Name: _____

Date: _____

Class: _____

Accents

A or G

1. nuevos _____ _____
2. Carlos _____ _____
3. Chacon _____ _____
4. padre _____ _____
5. frances _____ _____
6. escritorio _____ _____
7. Andres _____ _____
8. joven _____ _____
9. despues _____ _____
10. amistad _____ _____
11. tiendas _____ _____
12. personalidad _____ _____
13. aqui _____ _____
14. feliz _____ _____
15. superior _____ _____
16. adios _____ _____
17. secretaria _____ _____
18. violin _____ _____
19. carreteras _____ _____
20. Galvan _____ _____

Exercise

The following *agudas* words have three syllables and require a written accent.

(Las siguientes palabras agudas tienen tres sílabas y requieren acento escrito.)

Name: _____

Date: _____

Class: _____

Read the words, divide into syllables, and apply the accent.

(Lea las palabras, divida en sílabas y agregue el acento.)

1. japones   ja   po (nés) _____
2. aleman   _____
3. corazon   _____
4. algodon   _____
5. ojala   _____
6. calcetin   _____
7. almacen   _____
8. pantalon   _____
9. cinturon   _____
10. ademas   _____
11. matine   _____
12. bailarin   _____

These words are called *Agudas*

Exercise

The following *agudas* words are verbs that have three or four syllables with the stress on the last syllable and require a written accent. They are in the preterite and future tenses.

(Las siguientes palabras agudas son verbos que tienen tres o cuatro sílabas con el énfasis en la última sílaba y requieren un acento escrito. Estas palabras se usan en los tiempos pretérito y futuro.)

These words are called *agudas*

3

Rule 3

Divide into syllables, circle the stressed syllable and apply the accent.
(**Divida en sílabas, rodee la sílaba que tenga el énfasis y aplique el acento.**

1.	hablare	ha bla (ré) _____	(I shall speak)
2.	escribi	_____	(I wrote)
3.	comeras	_____	(You will eat)
4.	viviran	_____	(They will live)
5.	comprare	_____	(I will buy)
6.	trabajo	_____	(He worked)
7.	abrira	_____	(He will open)
8.	venderas	_____	(You will sell)
9.	recibi	_____	(I received)
10.	estudiaras	_____	(You will study)
11.	saludare	_____	(I will greet)
12.	caminaran	_____	(They will walk)

Exercise
Spanish Names (Agudas)

Name: _____

Date: _____

Class: _____

The following Spanish names are *agudas*, words that have two, three, or four syllables and require a written accent.

(Los siguientes nombres en español son palabras agudas que tienen dos, tres, o cuatro sílabas y requieren un acento escrito.)

Divide the names into syllables and apply the accents.
(Divida los nombres en sílabas y aplique los acentos.)

1. Duran — Du rán _____
2. Guzman _____
3. Felan _____
4. Panama _____
5. Joaquin _____
6. Calderon _____
7. Agustin _____
8. Nicolas _____
9. Aleman _____
10. Benjamin _____
11. Castillon _____
12. Alarcon _____
13. Yucatan _____
14. Obregon _____
15. Michoacan _____

Accents Exercise

Write the following words, circle the stressed syllable, and add the accent if necessary.

(Escriba las palabras, rodee la sílaba con el enfasis y escriba el acento si es necesario.)

Name: _____

Date: _____

Class: _____

1. ingles _____
2. enfermedad _____
3. escribi _____
4. joven _____
5. capitan _____
6. general _____
7. Nicolas _____
8. plumas _____
9. adios _____
10. autobus _____
11. secretarias _____
12. Veracruz _____
13. caminaran _____
14. japones _____
15. televisor _____
16. corazon _____
17. pizarra _____
18. aleman _____
19. felicidad _____
20. ojala _____

3 | Rule 3

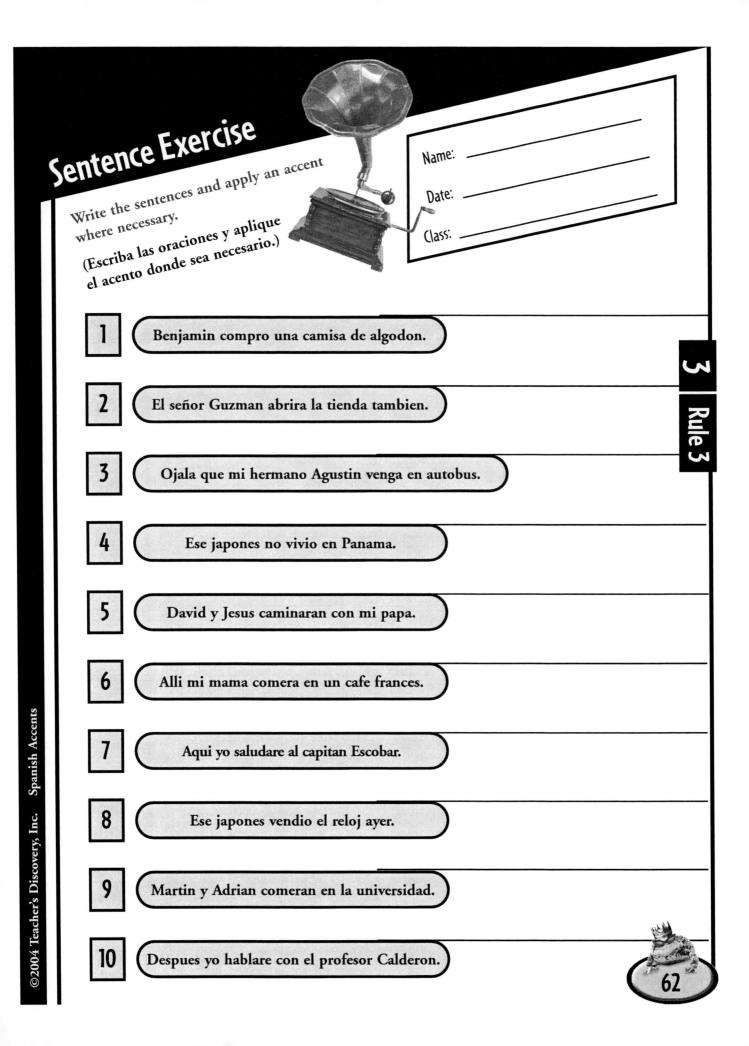

Sentence Exercise

Write the sentences and apply an accent where necessary.

(Escriba las oraciones y aplique el acento donde sea necesario.)

Name: _____

Date: _____

Class: _____

1 Benjamin compro una camisa de algodon.

2 El señor Guzman abrira la tienda tambien.

3 Ojala que mi hermano Agustin venga en autobus.

4 Ese japones no vivio en Panama.

5 David y Jesus caminaran con mi papa.

6 Alli mi mama comera en un cafe frances.

7 Aqui yo saludare al capitan Escobar.

8 Ese japones vendio el reloj ayer.

9 Martin y Adrian comeran en la universidad.

10 Despues yo hablare con el profesor Calderon.

Exercise
Word Identification

Add accents if necessary and identify all words as *agudas* or *graves*.

(Escriba los acentos si es necesario e identifique las palabras como agudas o graves.)

Name: _____

Date: _____

Class: _____

	A-Aguda	G-Grave

1. sillas   _____
2. recibi   _____
3. jardin   _____
4. nariz   _____
5. seran   _____
6. calcetin   _____
7. nacional   _____
8. Michoacan   _____
9. estudiaras   _____
10. papeles   _____
11. pantalon   _____
12. superior   _____
13. Andres   _____
14. padres   _____
15. Yucatan   _____
16. violin   _____
17. Ortiz   _____
18. mexicana   _____
19. almacen   _____
20. Leticia   _____

Exercise
Paragraphs with Accents

These paragraphs contain words that do require a written accent.

(Estos párrafos contienen palabras que sí requieren un acento escrito.)

Read the paragraphs and apply accents if necessary.

(Lea los párrafos y aplique acentos si son necesarios.)

El profesor Alarcon enseña español y frances en la universidad. Alli asisten Ines y Jose. Ellos estudian ingles. Yo estudiare español. Mañana yo ire a hablar con el director Cantu.

Mi hermano Ruben trabaja en un almacen. Alli tiene que saber ingles y tambien tiene que usar una camisa y un pantalon azul. El dueño es japones y vivio en Yucatan. Ojala sean amigos.

Test

Write the words, add the accent if necessary, and identify as *agudas* or *graves*.

(Escriba las palabras, aplique el acento si es necesario e identifique como agudas o graves.)

Name:_____

Date:_____

Class:_____

Accents

A or G

1.	nacional	
2.	bailarin	
3.	familia	
4.	vendio	
5.	estudiare	
6.	Gabriel	
7.	ojala	
8.	calculador	
9.	Diana	
10.	Castillon	
11.	Veracruz	
12.	corazon	
13.	apartamentos	
14.	jardin	
15.	Adrian	
16.	central	
17.	viviran	
18.	felicidad	
19.	Nicolas	
20.	Isabel	

Accents
Rule 4

Words that end in a consonant, except *n* or *s*, with a stress on the next-to-the-last syllable, require a written accent.

Las palabras que terminan con una consonante, excepto *n* o *s* y tienen el énfasis en la penúltima sílaba, requieren acento escrito.

Name: _____

Date: _____

Class: _____

These words are called *graves*

(pencil)
(easy)
(sugar)

Examples:
1. lápiz
2. fácil
3. azúcar

lá piz
fá cil
a zú car

Exercise

Graves words that end in a consonant, except *n* or *s*, with a stress on the next-to-the-last syllable require a written accent.

(Las palabras graves que terminan con una consonante, excepto *n* o *s* y tienen el énfasis en la penúltima sílaba, requieren un acento escrito.)

These words are called *graves*.

3 | **Rule 3**

Divide into syllables, circle the stressed syllable and apply the accent.
Divida en sílabas, rodee la sílaba que tenga el énfasis y aplique el acento.

1.	dolar	(dó) lar _____	(dollar)
2.	arbol	_____	(tree)
3.	angel	_____	(angel)
4.	util	_____	(useful)
5.	huesped	_____	(guest)
6.	carcel	_____	(jail)
7.	lider	_____	(leader)
8.	debil	_____	(weak)
9.	sueter	_____	(sweater)
10.	cancer	_____	(cancer)
11.	futbol	_____	(soccer, football)
12.	beisbol	_____	(baseball)

Optional Test

Write the words, add the accent if necessary, and identify as *agudas* or *graves*.

(Escriba las palabras, aplique el acento si es necesario e identifique como agudas o graves.)

Name: _____
Date: _____
Class: _____

Accents

A or G

1. Duran _____ _____
2. recibi _____ _____
3. hermosa _____ _____
4. violin _____ _____
5. nariz _____ _____
6. tambien _____ _____
7. libertad _____ _____
8. millon _____ _____
9. bonitas _____ _____
10. joven _____ _____
11. autobus _____ _____
12. calles _____ _____
13. pantalon _____ _____
14. natural _____ _____
15. Panama _____ _____
16. calcetin _____ _____
17. ciudad _____ _____
18. pluma _____ _____
19. algodon _____ _____
20. mujer _____ _____

Exercise
Spanish Names

The following Spanish names are *graves* words that have two syllables and require a written accent.

(Los siguientes nombres en español son palabras Graves que tienen dos sílabas y requieren acento escrito.)

Divide the names into syllables and apply the accents.
(Divida los nombres en sílabas y aplique los acentos.)

1. Gomez   Gó mez _____

2. Lopez _____

3. Perez _____

4. Cesar _____

5. Hector _____

6. Victor _____

7. Chavez _____

8. Juarez _____

9. Sanchez _____

10. Mendez _____

11. Vasquez _____

12. Nañez _____

13. Velez _____

14. Marquez _____

15. Muzquiz _____

Accents Exercise

Write the following words, circle the stressed syllable, and add the accent if necessary.

(Escriba las palabras, rodee la sílaba con el énfasis y escriba el acento si es necesario.)

Name: _____

Date: _____

Class: _____

3 | Rule 3

1. familias _____
2. angel _____
3. plural _____
4. algodon _____
5. plumas _____
6. Josefina _____
7. almacen _____
8. inteligente _____
9. carcel _____
10. nariz _____
11. jardin _____
12. libertad _____
13. huesped _____
14. mujer _____
15. Marisol _____
16. sueter _____
17. Agustin _____
18. futbol _____
19. director _____
20. Mendez _____

Sentence Exercise

Write the sentences and apply an accent where necessary.

(Escriba las oraciones y aplique acento donde sea necesario.)

©2004 Teacher's Discovery, Inc.   Spanish Accents

Name: _____

Date: _____

Class: _____

3 | Rule 3

1 Ayer yo escribi con mi lapiz.

2 Andres compro un sueter por un dolar.

3 Joaquin le dijo adios a Ines.

4 El capitan Vasquez vendera su mesa grande.

5 Mi papa abrira la puerta del autobus.

6 Javier y Hector caminaran por aqui hoy.

7 La salud del señor Sanchez es muy debil.

8 Victor hablaba con el lider en el jardin.

9 Cesar estaba en la carcel de la ciudad.

10 Es muy facil comprar este sofa frances.

71

Exercise
Word Identification

Identify all words as *agudas* or *graves* and apply an accent where necessary

(Identifique las palabras como agudas o graves y aplique un acento donde sea necesario.)

	A-Aguda	G-Grave

1. corazon _____
2. inteligentes _____
3. beisbol _____
4. ciudad _____
5. Esquivel _____
6. huesped _____
7. Adrian _____
8. universidad _____
9. arbol _____
10. reloj _____
11. Evangelina _____
12. algodon _____
13. Juarez _____
14. secretaria _____
15. Ortiz _____
16. comprare _____
17. Carlos _____
18. util _____
19. Eduardo _____
20. ferrocarril _____

Exercise
Paragraphs with Accents

These paragraphs contain words that do require a written accent.

(Estos párrafos contienen palabras que sí requieren un acento escrito.)

Read the paragraphs and apply accents if necessary.

(Lea los párrafos y aplique acentos si son necesarios.)

Aqui trabaja el profesor Cesar Lopez. Su esposa Olga es profesora tambien. Ellos enseñan frances y aleman. Ellos dicen que despues quieren ir a vivir a San Francisco. Alli viviran con la mama de ella.

Ayer yo hable con el papa de Ruben. Me dijo que la semana pasada vendio unos zapatos color cafe. Tambien me dijo que con ese dinero compro un pantalon de algodon y un cinturon muy bonito.

Test

Write the words, add the accent if necessary, and identify as *agudas* or *graves*.

(Escriba las palabras, aplique el acento si es necesario e identifique como agudas o graves.)

Name: _____

Date: _____

Class: _____

A or G

Accents

1. almacen   _____   _____
2. Antonio   _____   _____
3. arbol   _____   _____
4. hospital   _____   _____
5. comeras   _____   _____
6. Benjamin   _____   _____
7. joven   _____   _____
8. Samuel   _____   _____
9. Perez   _____   _____
10. calcetin   _____   _____
11. cancer   _____   _____
12. Esteban   _____   _____
13. superior   _____   _____
14. Mendez   _____   _____
15. Yucatan   _____   _____
16. americanos   _____   _____
17. futbol   _____   _____
18. Guadalupe   _____   _____
19. autobus   _____   _____
20. huesped   _____   _____

Exercise

These *graves* words of three or four syllables have the stress on the next-to-the-last syllable and require a written accent.

(Estas palabras graves de tres o cuatro sílabas tienen el énfasis en la penúltima sílaba y requieren un acento escrito.)

These words are called *graves*

Divide into syllables, circle the stressed syllable, and write the accent.
(Divida en sílabas, rodee la sílaba que tenga el énfasis y escriba el acento.)

1. azucar   a (zú) car _____ (sugar)
2. dificil   _____ (difficult)
3. caracter   _____ (character)
4. inutil   _____ (useless)
5. esteril   _____ (sterile)
6. inmovil   _____ (unmovable)
7. revolver   _____ (revolver)
8. cadaver   _____ (corpse)
9. inhabil   _____ (unskillful)
10. automovil   _____ (automobile)

Exercise
Spanish Names (Graves)

The following Spanish names are *graves* words that have two and three syllables and require a written accent.

(Los siguientes nombres en español son palabras graves que tienen dos y tres sílabas y requieren un acento escrito.)

Divide the names into syllables and apply the accents.

(Divida los nombres en sílabas y aplique los acentos.)

1. Suarez   Suá)rez _____
2. Nuñez   _____
3. Ramirez   _____
4. Jimenez   _____
5. Ibañez   _____
6. Cristobal   _____
7. Hernandez   _____
8. Rodriguez   _____
9. Martinez   _____
10. Velasquez   _____
11. Fernandez   _____
12. Gonzalez   _____
13. Dominguez   _____
14. Gutierrez   _____
15. Melendrez   _____

Accents Exercise

Divide the following words, into syllables circle the stressed syllable, and add the accent if necessary.

(Divida las palabras, en sílabas rodee la sílaba con el énfasis y escriba el acento si es necesario.)

Name: _____

Date: _____

Class: _____

1. capitan _____
2. enfermedad _____
3. caracter _____
4. vendio _____
5. central _____
6. Fernandez _____
7. aleman _____
8. administrador _____
9. carcel _____
10. autobus _____
11. Andres _____
12. Angel _____
13. joven _____
14. Martinez _____
15. escritorio _____
16. azucar _____
17. escribi _____
18. nariz _____
19. Chavez _____
20. David _____

4 | Rule 4

Sentence Exercise

Write the sentences and apply an accent where necessary.

(Escriba las oraciones y aplique un acento donde sea necesario.)

4 | Rule 4

1. La tienda de Omar Gonzalez vendio todo el azucar.

2. El capitan compro un revolver aleman.

3. Mi hermano Victor juega beisbol y futbol.

4. El lider frances no habla ingles ni español.

5. Raquel Ramirez limpia su automovil nuevo.

6. Es muy difícil tener un jardin con muchas flores.

7. Su mama tiene el corazon muy debil.

8. Ese huesped japones tiene un caracter muy bueno.

9. El viaje de Jesus a Panama es inutil.

10. Martin Rodriguez escribe con lapiz tambien.

Exercise
Word Identification

Add accents if necessary and identify all words as *agudas* or *graves*.

(Escriba los acentos si son necesarios e identifique las palabras como agudas o graves.)

Name: _____

Date: _____

Class: _____

	A-Aguda	G-Grave

1. esteril _____

2. capital _____

3. util _____

4. cancer _____

5. Leticia _____

6. despues _____

7. Gutierrez _____

8. feliz _____

9. bailarin _____

10. Maximiliano _____

11. facil _____

12. Calderon _____

13. abri _____

14. algodon _____

15. Vasquez _____

16. libertad _____

17. Antonio _____

18. inmovil _____

19. Lopez _____

20. Castillon _____

4 | Rule 4

Exercise
Paragraph with Accents

These paragraphs contain words that do require a written accent.

(Estos párrafos contienen palabras que sí requieren acento escrito.)

Read the paragraphs and apply accents if necessary.

(Lea los párrafos y aplique acentos si son necesarios.)

Jose trabaja aqui. Vende camisas de algodon. Es muy dificil el trabajo porque el dueño es japones. Yo trabajo con Rene Dominguez. Nosotros vendemos un millon de pantalones cada año. Ojala tambien vendamos muchas camisas.

Mi amigo Cristobal vive por la calle Obregon. Es facil llegar a su casa. Vive cerca de la carcel. Alli vive con su mama y tienen un automovil nuevo. Tambien tienen un jardin con un arbol muy grande.

4 | Rule 4

True or False Test

Is the word correct? True or False!

(¿Está correcta la palabra? ¡Verdad o Falso!

| Name: |
| Date: |
| Class: |

V-Verdad   **F-Falso**

1.	cancér	V	F
2.	calcetín	V	F
3.	vendio	V	F
4.	nacional	V	F
5.	Gutiérrez	V	F
6.	cinturon	V	F
7.	ciudád	V	F
8.	céntral	V	F
9.	suéter	V	F
10.	Guadalupe	V	F
11.	Villarreal	V	F
12.	venderás	V	F
13.	almacén	V	F
14.	Andres	V	F
15.	Ortiz	V	F
16.	carreterás	V	F
17.	adios	V	F
18.	Pérez	V	F
19.	secretaria	V	F
20.	personalidád	V	F

Test

Write the words, add the accent if necessary, and identify as *aguda* or *grave*.

(Escriba las palabras, aplique el acento si es necesario e identifique como aguda o grave.

Name: _____

Date: _____

Class: _____

Accents

A or G

1. Javier
2. Joaquin
3. universidad
4. beisbol
5. Eduardo
6. despues
7. cadaver
8. violin
9. comprare
10. dificultad
11. Suarez
12. feliz
13. Nicolas
14. superior
15. ferrocarril
16. Fernandez
17. Francisco
18. dolar
19. Adrian
20. Sanchez

Optional Test

Write the words, add the accent if necessary, and identify as *agudas* or *graves*.

(Escriba las palabras, aplique el acento si es necesario e identifique como agudas o graves.)

Accents

A or G

4 | Rule 4

1. Jimenez _____ _____
2. azucar _____ _____
3. frances _____ _____
4. Lopez _____ _____
5. pesos _____ _____
6. angel _____ _____
7. Salvador _____ _____
8. vendio _____ _____
9. carcel _____ _____
10. jardin _____ _____
11. dificil _____ _____
12. Ramon _____ _____
13. azul _____ _____
14. Julio _____ _____
15. debil _____ _____
16. Martinez _____ _____
17. Marisol _____ _____
18. alli _____ _____
19. huesped _____ _____
20. japones _____ _____

Accents
Rule 5

Words that always stress the third (3rd) syllable from the end of the word require a written accent.

Las palabras que siempre tienen el énfasis en la antepenúltima sílaba requieren acento escrito.

These words are called *Esdrújulas*

Examples:
1. lápices
2. teléfono
3. automático

(lá) pi ces   (pencils)
te (lé) fo no   (telephone)
au to (má) ti co   (automatic)

Exercise

The following *Esdrújulas* words have three syllables and require a written accent.

(Las siguientes palabras esdrujúlas tienen tres sílabas y requieren acento escrito.)

Name: _____

Date: _____

Class: _____

These words are called *Esdrújulas*

Follow the example and apply the accent.
(Siga el ejemplo y aplique el acento.)

1. pajaro   (pá) ja ro _____ (bird)
2. medico   _____ (doctor)
3. musica   _____ (music)
4. numero   _____ (number)
5. platano   _____ (banana)
6. sabado   _____ (Saturday)
7. faciles   _____ (easy)
8. silaba   _____ (syllable)
9. maquina   _____ (machine)
10. jovenes   _____ (youngsters)
11. miercoles _____ (Wednesday)
12. dolares   _____ (dollars)

5 | Rule 5

©2004 Teacher's Discovery, Inc.   Spanish Accents

85

Exercise

Spanish Names (Esdrújulas)

Name: _____

Date: _____

Class: _____

The following spanish names are *Esdrújulas* words that have three syllables and require a written accent.

(Los siguientes nombres en español son palabras esdrújulas que tienen tres sílabas y requieren un acento escrito.)

Divide the words, circle the stressed syllable, and apply the accent.

(Divida los nombres en sílabas, rodee la sílaba con el énfasis y aplique los acentos.)

1. Monica   (Mó) ni ca _____
2. Mexico _____
3. Davila _____
4. Cardenas _____
5. Merida _____
6. Cordova _____
7. Panfilo _____
8. Casares _____
9. Nelida _____
10. Candido _____

5 | Rule 5

Accents Exercise

Write and divide the following words, circle the stressed syllable, and add the accent if necessary.

(Escriba y divida las palabras, rodee la sílaba con el énfasis y escriba el acento si es necesario.)

1. salud _____
2. chocolate _____
3. maquina _____
4. pizarra _____
5. inutil _____
6. Castillon _____
7. lider _____
8. Armando _____
9. ademas _____
10. joven _____
11. felicidad _____
12. miercoles _____
13. abrira _____
14. angel _____
15. sillas _____
16. Monica _____
17. nariz _____
18. cinturon _____
19. arbol _____
20. hotel _____

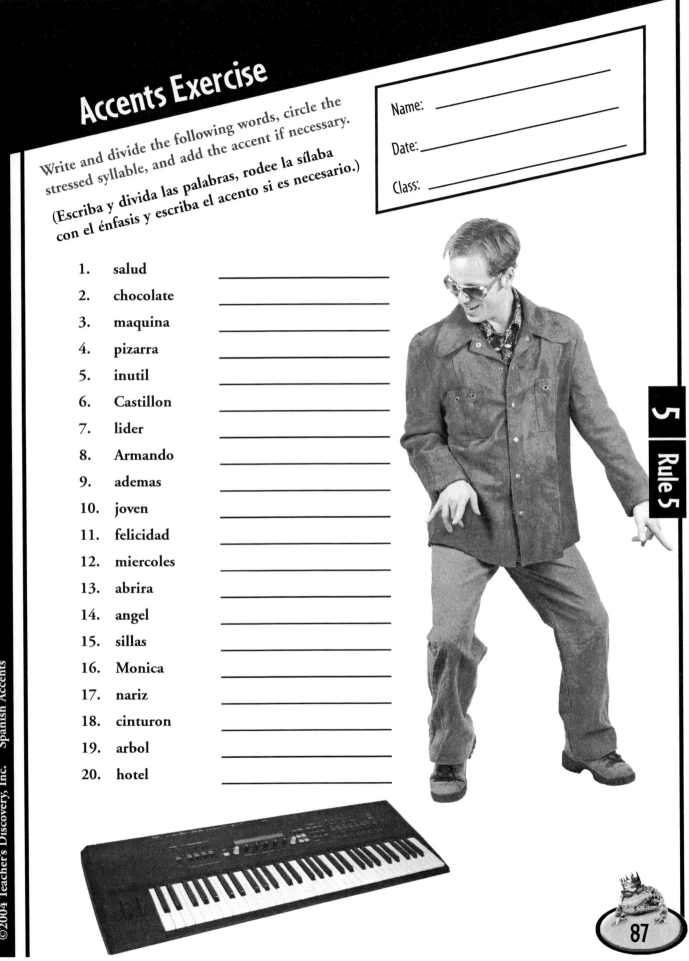

Sentence Exercise

Write the sentences and apply an accent where necessary.

(Escriba las oraciones y aplique acento donde sea necesario.)

Name:

Date:

Class:

Rule 5

1   Irma Casares compro este sofa por veinte dolares.

2   Yo no estudiare musica en la universidad.

3   La mama de Jesus abrira la oficina el sabado.

4   El capitan se llama Hector Davila.

5   Los jovenes juegan beisbol en Mexico.

6   Cesar es huesped en la casa del medico.

7   En el jardin estaba el pajaro de Joaquin.

8   Candido trabaja con la maquina numero tres.

9   Ramon y Nelida Venderán plumas y lapices.

10 El lider estaba en la carcel tambien.

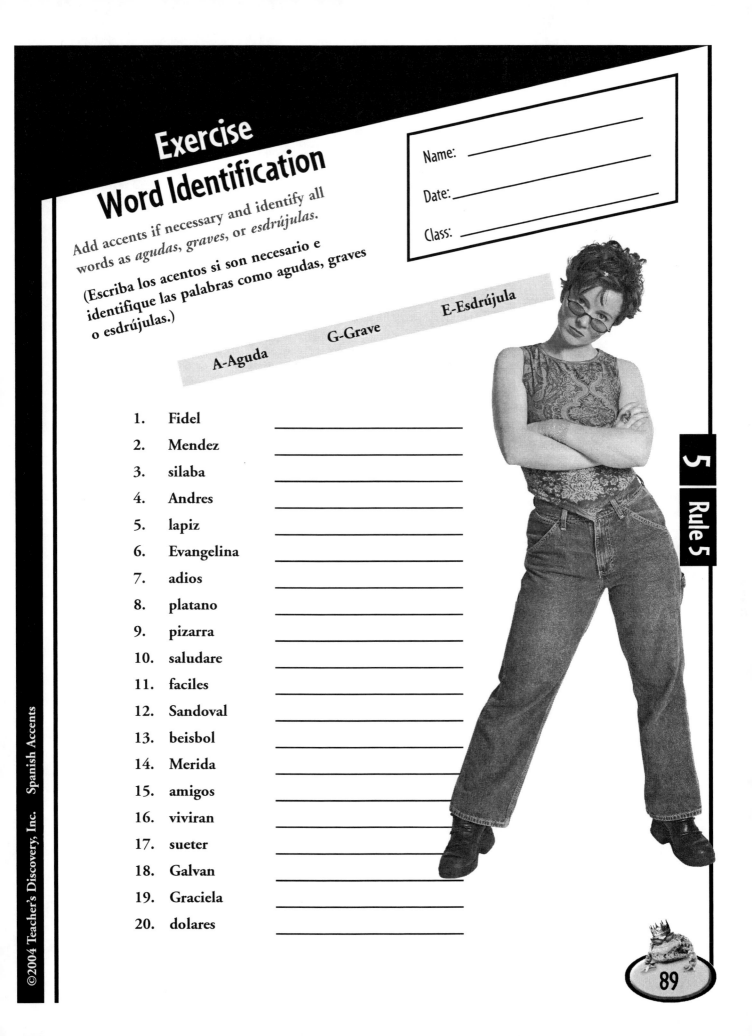

Exercise
Word Identification

Add accents if necessary and identify all words as *agudas, graves,* or *esdrújulas.*

(Escriba los acentos si son necesario e identifique las palabras como agudas, graves o esdrújulas.)

Name: _____

Date: _____

Class: _____

A-Aguda   G-Grave   E-Esdrújula

1. Fidel _____
2. Mendez _____
3. silaba _____
4. Andres _____
5. lapiz _____
6. Evangelina _____
7. adios _____
8. platano _____
9. pizarra _____
10. saludare _____
11. faciles _____
12. Sandoval _____
13. beisbol _____
14. Merida _____
15. amigos _____
16. viviran _____
17. sueter _____
18. Galvan _____
19. Graciela _____
20. dolares _____

Exercise
Paragraphs with Accents

These paragraphs contain words that do require a written accent.

(Estos párrafos contienen palabras que sí requieren acento escrito.)

Read the paragraphs and apply accents if necessary.

(Lea los párrafos y aplique acentos si son necesarios.)

Este miercoles Patricia comera en un cafe. Despues ira a su hotel. Vive en el cuarto numero dos. Alli vera a su novio Hector. Es profesor de ciencia en la Universidad de Mexico.

Ojala que los jovenes compren la maquina de escribir. La vendo por veinte dolares. Con ella yo escribi reportes muy dificiles en la clase de ingles. Mañana le comprare otra a Nicolas Cardenas.

5 | Rule 5

Test

Name: _____

Date: _____

Class: _____

Write the words, add the accent if necessary, and identify as *Agudas*, *Graves* or *Esdrújulas*.

(Escriba las palabras, aplique el acento si es necesario e identifique como agudas, graves o esdrújulas.

A, G, or E

Accents

#	Word	Accents	A, G, or E
1.	autobus		
2.	pajaros		
3.	enfermedad		
4.	cancer		
5.	hermanos		
6.	capitan		
7.	maquina		
8.	lider		
9.	superior		
10.	Alarcon		
11.	miercoles		
12.	Francisco		
13.	pantalon		
14.	numero		
15.	Jimenez		
16.	Raquel		
17.	dolar		
18.	abrira		
19.	Marquez		
20.	feliz		

5 | Rule 5

Exercise

These *Esdrújulas* words have four or five syllables and require a written accent.

(Estas palabras esdrújulas son de cuatro o cinco sílabas y requieren acento escrito.)

These words are called *Esdrújulas*

5 | Rule 5

Divide the words, circle the stressed syllable, and apply the accent.
(Divida las palabras, rodee la sílaba con el énfasis y aplique el acento.

1. mecanico   me (cá) ni co _____ (mechanic)
2. politica   _____ (politics)
3. hispanico   _____ (hispanic)
4. examenes   _____ (exams)
5. periodico   _____ (newspaper)
6. catolico   _____ (catholic)
7. historico   _____ (historic)
8. gramatica   _____ (grammar)
9. republica   _____ (republic)
10. democrata   _____ (democrat)
11. simpatico   _____ (nice)
12. matematica   _____ (mathematics)

Exercise

Spanish Names (Esdrújulas)

Name: _____

Date: _____

Class: _____

The following Spanish names are *esdrújulas* words that have four syllables and require a written accent.

(Los siguientes nombres en español son palabras esdrújulas que tienen cuatro sílabas y requieren un acento escrito.)

Divide the names into syllables and apply the accents.

(Divida los nombres en sílabas y aplique los acentos.)

1. America   A mé ri ca _____
2. Veronica   _____
3. Erendida   _____
4. Sepulveda   _____
5. Queretaro   _____
6. Geronimo   _____
7. Hipolito   _____
8. Angelica   _____
9. Pacifico   _____
10. Atlantico   _____

Exercise
Spanish Names (with Capital Letters)

Name: _____

Date: _____

Class: _____

These Spanish names are *graves* and *esdrújulas* words and require a written accent on the capital letter.

(Los siguientes nombres en español son palabras graves y esdrújulas y requieren acento escrito en la letra mayúscula)

Divide the words, circle the stressed syllable, and apply the accent.

(Divida las palabras, rodee la sílaba con el énfasis y aplique el acento.

1. Oscar   (Os) car _____
2. Africa   _____
3. Avila   _____
4. Angel   _____
5. Angeles   _____
6. Angulo   _____
7. Alvarez   _____
8. Iñiguez   _____
9. Aguila   _____
10. Avalos   _____

(NOTA: La Real Academia Española ha dispuesto que las letras mayúsculas lleven el acento que las reglas generales exijan.)

NOTE: The Real Academia Española decided that capital letters be accented as required by general rules.

Accents Exercise

Write the following words and add the accent if necessary.

(Escriba las siguientes palabras y escriba el acento si es necesario.)

1. cartas _____
2. esteril _____
3. matematica _____
4. ferrocarril _____
5. jardin _____
6. joven _____
7. Pacifico _____
8. caracter _____
9. viviran _____
10. pizarra _____
11. Velasquez _____
12. residencial _____
13. catolico _____
14. carcel _____
15. Carmen _____
16. algodon _____
17. automovil _____
18. pajaro _____
19. enfermedad _____
20. Tomas _____

Sentence Exercise

Write the sentences and apply an accent where necessary.

(Escriba las oraciones y aplique acento donde sea necesario.)

Name: _____

Date: _____

Class: _____

1 El mecanico compro un carro por cien dolares.

2 Oscar es el lider de los democratas.

3 Yo escribi los examenes faciles.

4 El periodico americano es de Veronica Muzquiz.

5 La gramatica del ingles no es facil.

6 Jose Gonzalez vivio cerca del Pacífico.

7 La Republica de Mexico tiene una carretera historica.

8 El joven simpatico hablo por telefono.

9 Mi hermano Ramon juega beisbol en Queretaro.

10 Los jovenes catolicos no son politicos.

5

Rule 5

Exercise
Word Identification

Add accents if necessary and identify all words as *agudas*, *graves*, or *esdrújulas*.

(Escriba los acentos si son necesarios e identifique las palabras como agudas, graves, o esdrújulas.)

Name: _____

Date: _____

Class: _____

A-Aguda	G-Grave	E-Esdrújula

1. nacional _____
2. hispanico _____
3. presidente _____
4. jardin _____
5. sueter _____
6. platano _____
7. Cristobal _____
8. calculador _____
9. papeles _____
10. Esquivel _____
11. azucar _____
12. Angelica _____
13. libertad _____
14. inteligente _____
15. matematica _____
16. comi _____
17. esteril _____
18. automatico _____
19. central _____
20. Atlantico _____

5 | Rule 5

Exercise
Paragraphs with Accents

These paragraphs contain words that do require a written accent.

(Estos párrafos contienen palabras que sí requieren acento escrito.)

Read the paragraphs and apply accents if necessary.

(Lea los párrafos y aplique acentos si son necesarios.)

El señor Fernadez es un democrata. El sabado tiene una junta politica. Alli hablan por telefono con representantes de la Republica de Mexico. El capitan Davila es el presidente del grupo.

El carro de Andres es automatico. Lo compro nuevo por cinco mil dolares. Mi hermano Agustin es mecanico y dice que el carro es bueno. Mi mama quiere comprar uno tambien. El miercoles ira a ver uno.

5 | Rule 5

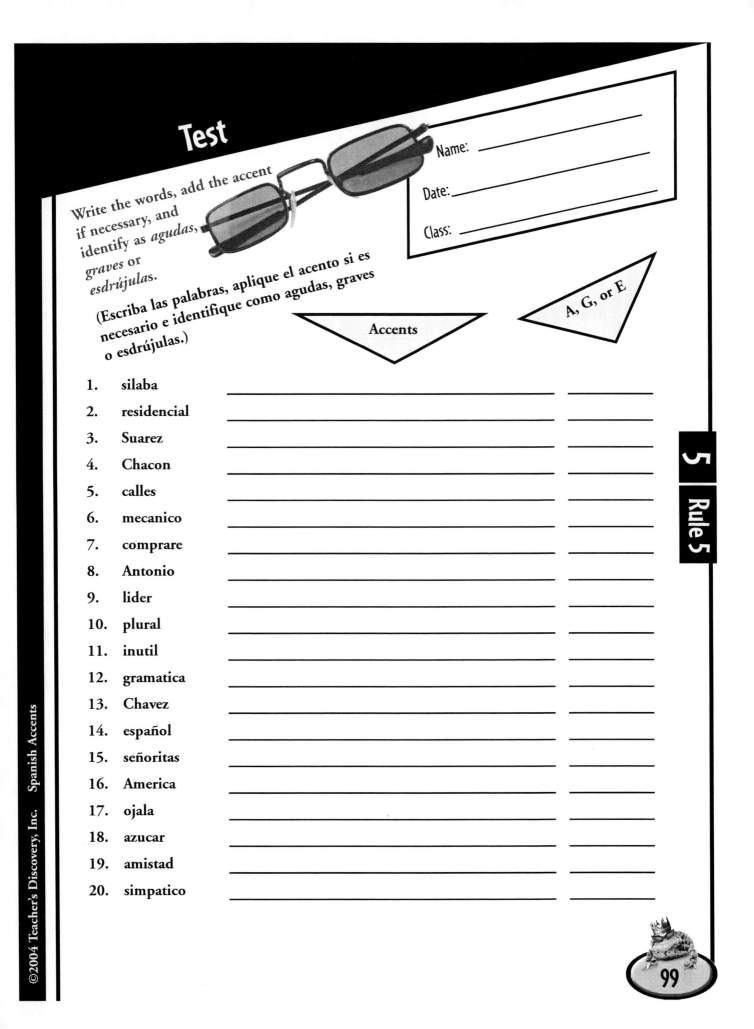

Test

Write the words, add the accent if necessary, and identify as *agudas*, *graves* or *esdrújulas*.

(Escriba las palabras, aplique el acento si es necesario e identifique como agudas, graves o esdrújulas.)

Name: _____

Date: _____

Class: _____

Accents

A, G, or E

1. silaba _____ _____
2. residencial _____ _____
3. Suarez _____ _____
4. Chacon _____ _____
5. calles _____ _____
6. mecanico _____ _____
7. comprare _____ _____
8. Antonio _____ _____
9. lider _____ _____
10. plural _____ _____
11. inutil _____ _____
12. gramatica _____ _____
13. Chavez _____ _____
14. español _____ _____
15. señoritas _____ _____
16. America _____ _____
17. ojala _____ _____
18. azucar _____ _____
19. amistad _____ _____
20. simpatico _____ _____

Accents
Rule 6

Words that end in *ion* (*cion, sion, nion, etc.*) always stress on the last syllable and require a written accent on the vowel *o*.

Las palabras que terminan en "ion" (cion, sion, nion, etc.) siempre tienen el énfasis en al última sílaba y requieren acento escrito en la vocal o.

These words are called *Agudas*

Examples:
1. nación   na ⟨ción⟩   (nation)
2. religión   re li ⟨gión⟩   (religion)
3. televisión   te le vi ⟨sión⟩   (television)

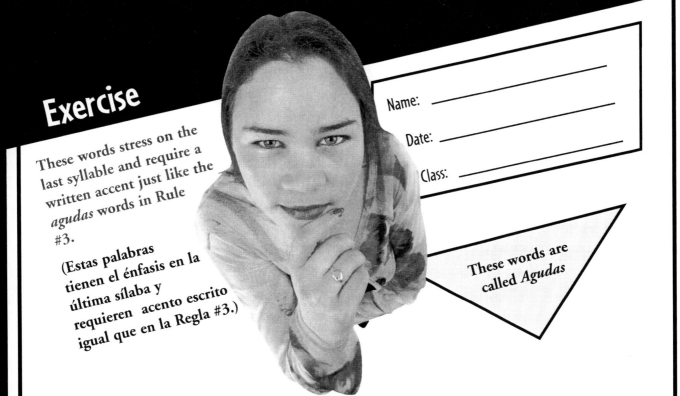

Exercise

These words stress on the last syllable and require a written accent just like the *agudas* words in Rule #3.

(Estas palabras tienen el énfasis en la última sílaba y requieren acento escrito igual que en la Regla #3.)

These words are called *Agudas*

6 | Rule 6

Follow the example and apply the accent.
(**Siga el ejemplo y aplique el acento.**)

1.	leccion	lec ción _____	(lesson)
2.	avion	_____	(airplane)
3.	region	_____	(region)
4.	union	_____	(union)
5.	cancion	_____	(song)
6.	mision	_____	(mission)
7.	accion	_____	(action)
8.	pasion	_____	(passion)
9.	pension	_____	(pension)
10.	mencion	_____	(mention)
11.	mansion	_____	(mansion)
12.	locion	_____	(lotion)

Accents Exercise

Write the following words and add the accent if necessary.

(Escriba las siguientes palabras y escriba el acento si es necesario.)

1. ciudad _____
2. mision _____
3. dificil _____
4. Mexico _____
5. historico _____
6. locion _____
7. administrador _____
8. inutil _____
9. escribi _____
10. Gonzalez _____
11. ingles _____
12. hijos _____
13. almacen _____
14. accion _____
15. examenes _____
16. familias _____
17. Atlantico _____
18. Perez _____
19. abrira _____
20. humanidad _____

6 | Rule 6

Write the sentences and apply an accent where necessary.

(Escriba las oraciones y aplique acento donde sea necesario.)

1 La leccion de frances no es dificil.

2 Ojala que mi papa hable con el señor Vasquez.

3 Los jovenes tambien vienen por avion.

4 Los mecanicos trabajan en esta region.

5 El musico toca mi cancion favorita.

6 Los democratas se juntan aqui en esta mansion.

7 Veronica trabaja con Jesus todos los miercoles.

8 El lider de la nacion es Hector Galvan.

9 Angel Juarez es presidente de la union.

10 Nelida Ramirez tiene una pension.

Exercise
Word Identification

Add accents if necessary and identify all words as *agudas*, *graves*, or *esdrújulas*.

(Escriba los acentos si son necesarios e identifique las palabras como agudas, graves o esdrújulas.)

A-Aguda	G-Grave	E-Esdrújula

1. escritorio _____
2. corazon _____
3. maquina _____
4. caracter _____
5. mencion _____
6. Nuñez _____
7. tiendas _____
8. calcetin _____
9. gramatica _____
10. venderas _____
11. ciudad _____
12. sueter _____
13. dificultad _____
14. Muzquiz _____
15. medicos _____
16. pasion _____
17. hermosa _____
18. Pacifico _____
19. futbol _____
20. capitan _____

6 | Rule 6

104

Exercise
Paragraphs with Accents

These paragraphs contain words that do require a written accent.

(Estos párrafos contienen palabras que sí requieren acento escrito.)

Read the paragraphs and apply accents if necessary.

(Lea los párrafos y aplique acentos si son necesarios.)

Mi hermano Adrian dice que Veronica le dijo que la leccion de ingles no es dificil. En esta region, todas las escuelas tambien enseñan frances. Todos dicen que los examenes son faciles.

Rene Chavez trabajo con la union local numero 654. Ganaba mil dolares por semana. Ahora recibe una pension muy buena. Con ese dinero compro una mansion muy grande. Alli vive muy feliz.

6

Rule 6

Test

Write the words, add the accent if necessary, and identify as *agudas, graves* or *esdrújulas.*

(Escriba las palabras, aplique el acento si es necesario e identifique como agudas, graves o esdrújulas.)

Name: _____

Date: _____

Class: _____

Accents

A, G or E

1. huesped _____ _____

2. libertad _____ _____

3. platano _____ _____

4. Guzman _____ _____

5. Martinez _____ _____

6. escribi _____ _____

7. republica _____ _____

8. padres _____ _____

9. azucar _____ _____

10. cancion _____ _____

11. Suarez _____ _____

12. pajaro _____ _____

13. pizarra _____ _____

14. ademas _____ _____

15. salud _____ _____

16. hispanico _____ _____

17. comprare _____ _____

18. automovil _____ _____

19. nacion _____ _____

20. Francisco _____ _____

Exercise

This exercise has three, four, and five syllable words that end in *ion* (*cion, sion, nion,* etc.) with a stress on the last syllable and require a written accent on the vowel *o*.

Este ejercicio tiene palabras de tres, cuatro, y cinco sílabas que terminan en "ion" (cion, sion, nion, etc.) y tienen el énfasis en la última sílaba y requieren acento escrito en la vocal *o*.)

These words are called *Agudas*

6

Rule 6

Divide into syllables, circle the stressed syllable and apply the accent.
(Divida en sílabas, rodee la sílaba que tenga el énfasis y aplique el accento.)

1. opinion   o pi (nión) _____ (opinion)
2. direccion   _____ (direction)
3. poblacion   _____ (population)
4. eleccion   _____ (election)
5. confesion   _____ (confession)
6. condicion   _____ (condition)
7. explicacion   _____ (explanation)
8. generacion   _____ (generation)
9. contestacion   _____ (answer)
10. comparacion   _____ (comparison)
11. desesperacion _____ (desperation)
12. administracion _____ (administration)

Exercise
Spanish Names (Agudas)

The following Spanish names are *agudas* words that end in *ión* and require a written accent.

(Los siguientes nombres en español son palabras agudas que terminan en "ión" y requieren acento escrito.)

Divide the nouns into syllables, circle the stressed syllable and apply the accents.

(**Divida los nombres en sílabas, rodee la sílaba con el énfasis y aplique los acentos.**)

1. Concepcion   Con cep (ción) _____
2. Asuncion   _____
3. Encarnacion   _____
4. Carrion   _____

Other Nouns

(**Otros nombres**)

1. Constitucion _____
2. Migracion _____
3. Gobernacion _____
4. Supervision _____
5. Administracion _____
6. Inspeccion _____

©2004 Teacher's Discovery, Inc.   Spanish Accents

6 | Rule 6

108

Write the following words and add the accent if necessary.

(Escriba las siguientes palabras y escriba el acento si es necesario.)

Name: _____

Date: _____

Class: _____

1. faciles _____
2. debil _____
3. union _____
4. miercoles _____
5. universidad _____
6. perros _____
7. comparacion _____
8. reloj _____
9. democrata _____
10. angel _____
11. Calderon _____
12. señor _____
13. almacen _____
14. eleccion _____
15. arbol _____
16. telefonos _____
17. televisor _____
18. autobus _____
19. poblacion _____
20. Melendrez _____

6

Rule 6

Write the sentences and apply an accent where necessary.

(Escriba las oraciones y aplique acento donde sea necesario.)

Name: _____

Date: _____

Class: _____

1 Jose Lopez tiene mi contestacion.

2 El papa de Jesus trabaja con la administracion.

3 La clase de Frances no tiene supervision.

4 El lider de los democratas es Andres Carrion.

5 La Migracion vino por Hector Fernandez.

6 El profesor Velez tiene una explicacion.

7 Encarnacion trabajo en el Departamento de Inspeccion.

8 Agustin Rodriguez es un catolico bueno.

9 Los examenes de la clase de religion son faciles.

10 Victor compro una television nueva.

Exercise
Word Identification

Add accents if necessary and identify all words as *agudas, graves,* or *esdrújulas.*

(Escriba los acentos si son necesarios e identifique las palabras como agudas, graves, o esdrújulas.)

Name: _____

Date: _____

Class: _____

6 | Rule 6

A-Aguda	G-Grave	E-Esdrújula

1. general   _____
2. confesion   _____
3. dificil   _____
4. Monica   _____
5. secretaria   _____
6. aleman   _____
7. historico   _____
8. cancer   _____
9. comeras   _____
10. joven   _____
11. lapices   _____
12. algodon   _____
13. poblacion   _____
14. automatico   _____
15. carcel   _____
16. sabado   _____
17. huesped   _____
18. Marisol   _____
19. accion   _____
20. calles   _____

111

Exercise
Paragraphs with Accents

These paragraphs contain words that do require a written accent.

(Estos párrafos contienen palabras que sí requieren acento escrito.)

Read the paragraphs and apply accents if necessary.

(Lea los párrafos y aplique acentos si son necesarios.)

El señor Carrion y su esposa Carmen viven en el cuarto numero 5. La condicion del hotel no es buena. Tiene un sofa chico. Tambien tiene una television con el color debil. Ellos viviran alli un año.

Nicolas Martinez recibio una carta de su prima Nelida con cien dolares. Con ese dinero llevo a su novia Concepcion a comer a un restaurante. Despues le compro un perfume y una locion muy buena.

Test

©2004 Teacher's Discovery, Inc.   Spanish Accents

Write the words, add the accent if necessary, and identify as *agudas*, *graves*, or *esdrújulas*.

(Escriba las palabras, aplique el acento si es necesario e identifique como agudas, graves o esdrújulas.)

Name: _____

Date: _____

Class: _____

Accents

A, G or e

6

Rule 6

		Accents	A, G or e
1.	sueter	_____	_____
2.	Casares	_____	_____
3.	universidad	_____	_____
4.	adios	_____	_____
5.	desesperacion	_____	_____
6.	televisor	_____	_____
7.	pajaro	_____	_____
8.	Antonio	_____	_____
9.	angel	_____	_____
10.	aleman	_____	_____
11.	lecciones	_____	_____
12.	hablare	_____	_____
13.	simpatico	_____	_____
14.	Gonzalez	_____	_____
15.	inspeccion	_____	_____
16.	familia	_____	_____
17.	republica	_____	_____
18.	dificil	_____	_____
19.	mision	_____	_____
20.	cancer	_____	_____

Words having a diphthong (two vowels together) that have a weak vowel and a strong vowel and produce two separate sounds, require a written accent on the weak vowel.

Las palabras que tienen un diptongo (dos vocales juntas) que consiste de una vocal débil y una vocal fuerte y produce dos sonidos separados, requieren un acento escrito en la vocal débil.

These words are called *Graves*

Examples:
1. tío   (tí) o   (uncle)
2. tenía   te (ní) a   (I had)
3. mayoría   ma yo (rí) a   (majority)

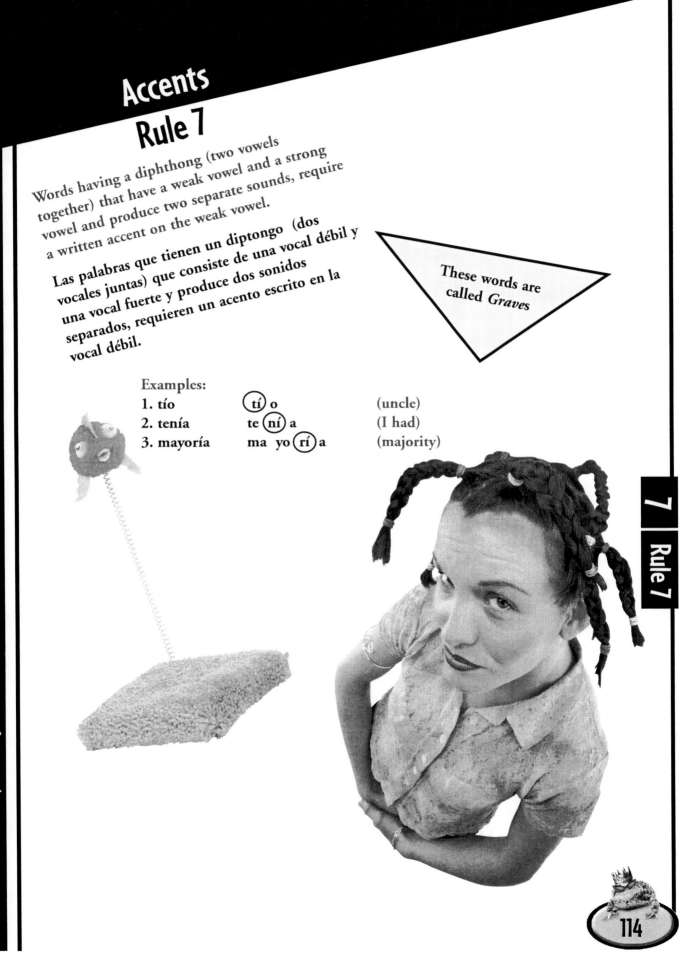

Exercise

The following exercise contains words that have a diphthong that produces two separate sounds and two syllables.

(El siguiente ejercicio contiene palabras que tienen un diptongo que produce dos sonidos separados y dos sílabas.)

These words are called *Graves*

Some of these words are used as verbs.
(Algunas de estas palabras se usan como verbos.)

Divide into syllables, circle the stressed syllable and add the necessary accent to separate the diphthong.
(Divida en sílabas, rodee la sílaba con el énfasis y escriba el acento necesario para separar el diptongo.)

1.	mio	(mi)o _____	(mine)	(m.)
2.	pais	_____	(country)	
3.	tia	_____	(aunt)	
4.	rio	_____	(river)	
5.	raiz	_____	(root)	
6.	mia	_____	(mine)	(f.)
7.	maiz	_____	(corn)	
8.	dia	_____	(day)	
9.	frio	_____	(cold)	
10.	comia	_____	(used to eat)	
11.	vivia	_____	(used to live)	
12.	corria	_____	(used to run)	

7 | Rule 7

©2004 Teacher's Discovery, Inc.   Spanish Accents

115

Exercise

Spanish Names with Diphthongs

Name: _____

Date: _____

Class: _____

These Spanish names have a diphthong that has a combination of a weak vowel and strong vowel and requires a written accent.

(Estos nombres en español tienen un diptongo que tiene una combinación de una vocal fuerte y una vocal débil y requiere un acento escrito.)

Divide the names into syllables, circle the stressed syllable and apply the accents.

(Divida los nombres en sílabas, rodee la sílaba con el énfasis y aplique los acentos.)

1. Diaz   (Dí) az _____
2. Rios   _____
3. Raul   _____
4. Aida   _____
5. Lucia   _____
6. Elias   _____
7. Saul   _____
8. Maria   _____
9. Sofia   _____
10. Rocio   _____

Accents Exercise

Write the following words and add the accent if necessary.

(Escriba las siguientes palabras y escriba el acento si es necesario.)

1. cancion   _____
2. Angeles   _____
3. ciudad   _____
4. automovil   _____
5. comia   _____
6. secretaria   _____
7. jardin   _____
8. Castillon   _____
9. amistad   _____
10. bailarin   _____
11. medico   _____
12. Aida   _____
13. reloj   _____
14. explicacion   _____
15. muchos   _____
16. lapiz   _____
17. maiz   _____
18. tambien   _____
19. poblacion   _____
20. venderas   _____

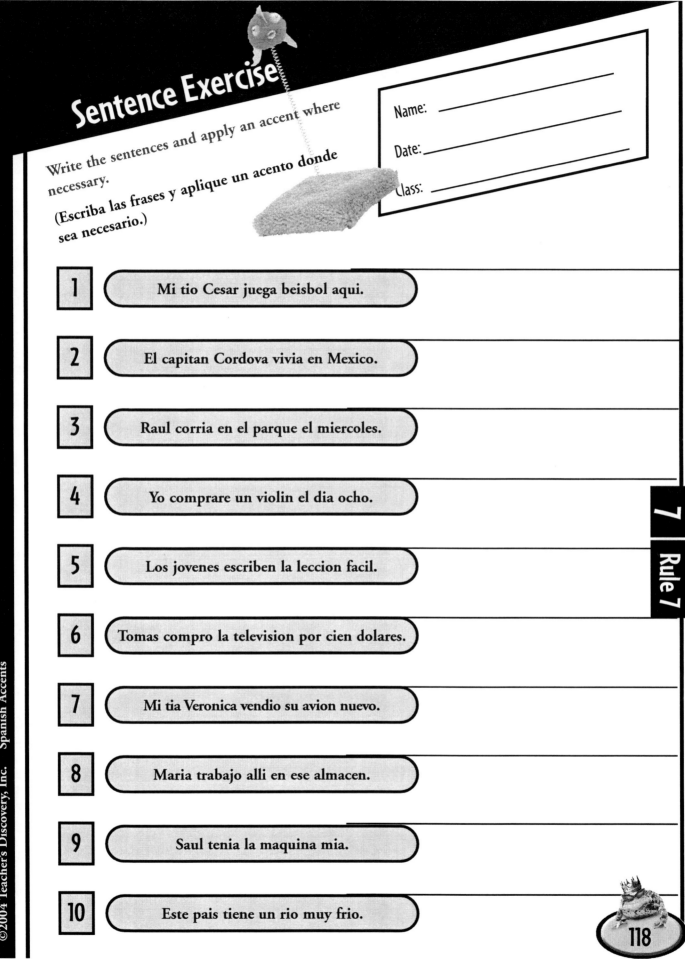

Sentence Exercise

Write the sentences and apply an accent where necessary.

(Escriba las frases y aplique un acento donde sea necesario.)

Name: _____

Date: _____

Class: _____

1 Mi tio Cesar juega beisbol aqui.

2 El capitan Cordova vivia en Mexico.

3 Raul corria en el parque el miercoles.

4 Yo comprare un violin el dia ocho.

5 Los jovenes escriben la leccion facil.

6 Tomas compro la television por cien dolares.

7 Mi tia Veronica vendio su avion nuevo.

8 Maria trabajo alli en ese almacen.

9 Saul tenia la maquina mia.

10 Este pais tiene un rio muy frio.

7

Rule 7

Exercise
Word Identification

Add accents if necessary and identify all words as *agudas, graves* or *esdrújulas.*

(Escriba los acentos si son necesarios e identifique las palabras como agudas, graves o esdrújulas.)

Name: _____

Date: _____

Class: _____

A-Aguda	G-Grave	E-Esdrújula

1. inutil _____
2. despues _____
3. telefono _____
4. corazon _____
5. Aguilar _____
6. mios _____
7. calcetin _____
8. sabado _____
9. Dominguez _____
10. administrador _____
11. autobus _____
12. mexicano _____
13. democrata _____
14. ojala _____
15. Raquel _____
16. arbol _____
17. Velasquez _____
18. musica _____
19. amigo _____
20. Nicolas _____

7 | Rule 7

119

Exercise
Paragraphs with Accents

Name: _____

Date: _____

Class: _____

These paragraphs contain words that do require a written accent.

(Estos párrafos contienen palabras que sí requieren un acento escrito.)

Read the paragraphs and apply accents if necessary.

(Lea los párrafos y aplique acentos si son necesarios.)

Los jovenes estudiaban la leccion de ingles en la casa de mi tio Jose. Era muy facil porque el libro tenia la explicacion completa. Ellos quieren estudiar mucho porque los examenes son el dia veinte.

Mi tio Ruben Escobar trabajo en esta ciudad. Todos los dias viajaba por autobus. Comia en un cafe cerca del rio. Los sabados y domingos no trabajaba porque se iba a ver los juegos de beisbol.

7 | Rule 7

Test

©2004 Teacher's Discovery, Inc.   Spanish Accents

Write the words, add the accent if necessary, and identify as agudas, graves or esdrújulas.

(Escriba las palabras, aplique el acento si es necesario e identifique como agudas, graves o esdrújulas.)

Name: _____

Date: _____

Class: _____

Accents

A, G or E

1. futbol _____ _____
2. Sofia _____ _____
3. silaba _____ _____
4. comeras _____ _____
5. inteligente _____ _____
6. politica _____ _____
7. tenia _____ _____
8. tambien _____ _____
9. Gabriel _____ _____
10. lapices _____ _____
11. contestacion _____ _____
12. periodico _____ _____
13. violin _____ _____
14. chocolates _____ _____
15. matine _____ _____
16. faciles _____ _____
17. mencion _____ _____
18. lapiz _____ _____
19. canciones _____ _____
20. Obregon _____ _____

Exercise

The following words have a diphthong that has a weak vowel and a strong vowel. The written accent is placed on the weak vowel.

(Las siguientes palabras tienen un diptongo que tiene una vocal débil y una vocal fuerte. El acento escrito se pone en la vocal débil.)

These words are called *Graves*

Divide into syllables and apply the accent on the weak vowel.
(**Divida en sílabas y aplique el acento en la vocal débil.**)

1. policia   po li (cí) a _____ (police)
2. libreria   _____ (book store)
3. loteria   _____ (lottery)
4. minoria   _____ (minority)
5. fruteria   _____ (fruit stand)
6. compañia   _____ (company)
7. escribia   _____ (used to write)
8. todavia   _____ (still)
9. economia   _____ (economy)
10. cafeteria   _____ (cafeteria)
11. filosofia   _____ (philosophy)
12. zapateria   _____ (shoe store)

7 | Rule 7

©2004 Teacher's Discovery, Inc.   Spanish Accents

This rule on diphthongs can be applied to verb conjugations in several tenses (imperfect tense, conditional tense, etc.) and to words that contain triphthongs three vowels together.)

Esta regla sobre diptongos se puede aplicar a conjugaciones de verbos en varios tiempos (imperfecto, condicional, etc.) y a palabras que contienen triptongos (tres vocales juntas.)

Diphthongs and Triphthongs

7

Rule 7

Triphthongs also have a written accent on the weak vowel.
(Triptongos también tienen acento en la vocal débil.)

Divide into syllables, circle the stressed syllable.
(Divida en sílabas y rodee la sílaba que tenga acento.)

1. debia   de (bí) a _____ (used to owe)
2. salia   _____ (used to go out)
3. vendia   _____ (used to sell)
4. asistia   _____ (used to attend)
5. leia   _____ (used to read)
6. veia   _____ (used to see)
7. reia   _____ (used to laugh)
8. aprenderia   _____ (would learn)
9. hablaria   _____ (would speak)
10. recibia   _____ (used to receive)
11. dariamos   _____ (would give)
12. volverian   _____ (would return)

123

Exercise
Names with Diphthongs and Triphthongs

These Spanish names have a diphthong or a triphthong and require a written accent.

(Estos nombres en español tienen un diptongo o un triptongo y requieren un acento escrito.)

Name: _____

Date: _____

Class: _____

Divide the names into syllables and apply the accents.
(Divida los nombres en sílabas y aplique los acentos.)

1. Garcia   Gar (cí) a _____
2. Mejia _____
3. Tobias _____
4. Farias _____
5. Macias _____
6. Matias _____
7. Efrain _____
8. Eloisa _____
9. Rosalia _____
10. Chavarria _____
11. Renteria _____
12. Zacarias _____
13. Escontrias _____
14. Echeverria _____
15. Isaias _____

7 | Rule 7

Accents Exercise

Write the following words and add the accent if necessary

(Escriba las siguientes palabras y escriba el acento si es necesario.)

Name: _____

Date: _____

Class: _____

1. azucar   _____
2. libreria   _____
3. religion   _____
4. calculador   _____
5. dolares   _____
6. familia   _____
7. japones   _____
8. lider   _____
9. felicidad   _____
10. compañia   _____
11. Vasquez   _____
12. ferrocarril   _____
13. zapateria   _____
14. automatico   _____
15. Alarcon   _____
16. papeles   _____

7 | Rule 7

Write the sentences and apply an accent where necessary.

(Escriba las oraciones y aplique el acento donde sea necesario.)

Name: _____

Date: _____

Class: _____

1 La economia de Mexico es muy debil.

2 Ramon veia a Maria todos los dias.

3 Mi tia Josefina vendia la maquina de escribir.

4 La mama de Raul leia el periodico.

5 El capitan Juarez era el lider de los policias.

6 La señora Martinez todavia no recibia los lapices.

7 Cesar siempre corria despues de Matias.

8 Este pais tenia muchas compañias de azucar.

9 Eloisa salia del almacen con Cristobal.

10 Mi tio Tomas vivira en mi casa.

Add accents if necessary and identify all words as *agudas*, *graves*, or *esdrújulas*.

(Escriba los acentos si son necesarios e identifique las palabras como agudas, graves o esdrújulas.)

Name: _____

Date: _____

Class: _____

A-Aguda	G-Grave	E-Esdrújula

1. gramatica _____
2. hermanos _____
3. loteria _____
4. ayer _____
5. platanos _____
6. capital _____
7. caracter _____
8. recibi _____
9. reia _____
10. Encarnacion _____
11. zapato _____
12. numeros _____
13. Gomez _____
14. automovil _____
15. Chavarria _____
16. supervision _____
17. hablaria _____
18. señoritas _____
19. catolico _____
20. raiz _____

7

Rule 7

Exercise
Paragraphs with Accents

These paragraphs contain words that do require a written accent

(Estos párrafos contienen palabras que sí requieren acento escrito.)

Read the paragraphs and apply accents if necessary.

(Lea los párrafos y aplique acentos si son necesarios.)

Victor Macias estudia la leccion de matematicas. Los problemas no son faciles. Mañana hablara con el profesor Hernandez y despues ira a la libreria. El miercoles y el jueves seran los examenes.

Mi tio Hector leia el periodico todos los dias. Alli veia los numeros de la loteria. El año pasado, recibio un millon de dolares. Despues compro una cafeteria y vende comida mexicana.

128

Test

Write the words, add the accent if necessary, and identify as *agudas, graves* or *esdrújulas*.

(Escriba las palabras, aplique el acento si es necesario e identifique como agudas, graves, o esdrújulas.)

Accents

A, G, or E

1. japones _____ _____
2. faciles _____ _____
3. Eduardo _____ _____
4. huesped _____ _____
5. reloj _____ _____
6. Atlantico _____ _____
7. inutil _____ _____
8. central _____ _____
9. zapatos _____ _____
10. democrata _____ _____
11. Sofia _____ _____
12. ojala _____ _____
13. americano _____ _____
14. abrira _____ _____
15. cadaver _____ _____
16. mujer _____ _____
17. Leticia _____ _____
18. dolares _____ _____
19. debil _____ _____
20. fruteria _____ _____

Accents
Rule 8

Accents are applied to words that are spelled the same and are pronounced the same but have different meanings. The accent may change an article to a pronoun, an adjective to a pronoun, etc.

(Los acentos se aplican a palabras que se deletrean y se pronuncian igual pero que tienen diferente significado. El acento puede cambiar un artículo a un pronombre, un adjetivo a un pronombre, etc.)

These words are called *diacríticas*.

Examples:
1. el   the   (article)
2. él   he, him   (pronoun)

These words are called *diacríticas.*
These words are spelled and pronounced exactly
the same. The accent makes the difference.

Las palabras llamadas diacríticas se escriben y
pronuncian exactamente igual. El acento hace la
diferencia.)

1.	tu	your	possessive adjective
	tú	you	pronoun
2.	se	himself (etc.)	reflexive pronoun
	sé	know	verb
3.	mi	my	possessive adjective
	mí	me	personal pronoun
4.	te	yourself	reflexive pronoun
	té	tea	noun
5.	si	if	conjunction
	sí	yes	adverb
6.	solo	alone	adjective
	sólo	only	adverb
7.	de	of, from	preposition
	dé	give	verb
8.	mas	but	conjunction
	más	more	adverb
9.	este	this	demonstrative adjective
	éste	this one	demonstrative pronoun
10.	aquel	that	demonstrative adjective
	aquél	that one	demonstrative pronoun

8 | Rule 8

Accents Exercise

Write the following words and add the accent if necessary.

(Escriba las siguientes palabras y escriba el acento si es necesario.)

Name: _____

Date: _____

Class: _____

1. carcel _____
2. politica _____
3. presidente _____
4. autobus _____
5. si _____ (adv.)
6. Patricia _____
7. minoria _____
8. mi _____ (pos adj.)
9. mencion _____
10. dificil _____
11. tenia _____
12. adios _____
13. se _____ (verb)
14. simpatico _____
15. pizarras _____
16. jardin _____
17. esteril _____
18. joven _____
19. este _____ (dem. pro.)
20. investigador _____

Write the sentences and apply an accent where necessary.

(Escriba las oraciones y aplique un acento donde sea necesario.)

Name: _____

Date: _____

Class: _____

1 Tu y tu tio Ramon viviran con el.

2 Este violin lo compro mi papa para mi.

3 Despues el vivio aqui.

4 Si, el lider hablara con Joaquin Gomez.

5 Mi mama compro mucho te en el almacen.

6 El japones comio mas que Monica.

7 El capitan dijo que este es mio.

8 Los jovenes compraran aquel.

9 Tu y el venderan tu sofa.

10 El señor Perez quiere que yo de un millon de dolares.

8

Rule 8

133

Exercise
Word Identification

Add accents if necessary and identify all
words as *agudas*, *graves* or *esdrujulas*.

(Escriba los acentos si son necesarios e
identifique las palabras como agudas, graves
o esdrújulas.)

Name: _____

Date: _____

Class: _____

A-Aguda	G-Grave	E-Esdrújula

1. estudiare _____
2. Garcia _____
3. el _____ (pro.)
4. sabado _____
5. vendio _____
6. dineros _____
7. doctor _____
8. tu _____ (pos. adj.)
9. difícil _____
10. democrata _____
11. aquel _____ (dem. adj.)
12. Javier _____
13. facil _____
14. si _____ (yes)
15. periodico _____
16. feliz _____
17. autobus _____
18. arbol _____
19. mi _____ (pro.)
20. platano _____

8 | Rule 8

Exercise
Paragraphs with Accents

These paragraphs contain words that do require a written accent.

(Estos párrafos contienen palabras que sí requieren un acento escrito.)

Name: _____

Date: _____

Class: _____

Read the paragraphs and apply accents if necessary.

(Lea los párrafos y aplique acentos si son necesarios.)

El profesor Casares dijo que antes el corria en el parque. Todos los dias salia en las tardes a correr. Ayer compro un sueter para mi. Quiere que yo corra con el en las noches. Yo no se si podre.

Mi papa vivio en Mexico hace cuatro años. Dice que el tenia una zapateria. Alli trabajaba tu tio Candido Fernandez tambien. Ellos vivian en un hotel cerca de una cafeteria.

8 | Rule 8

135

Test

Write the words, add the accent if necessary, and identify as *agudas, grave sor esdrujulas.*

(Escriba las palabras, aplique el acento si es necesario e identifique como agudas, graves o esdrújulas.

Name: _____

Date: _____

Class: _____

Accents

A, G or E

1. escribi _____ _____

2. tu vendes _____ _____ (adj./pron)

3. reloj _____ _____

4. futbol _____ _____

5. hispanico _____ _____

6. Chacon _____ _____

7. facil _____ _____

8. que yo de _____ _____ (verb)

9. calcetin _____ _____

10. padres _____ _____

11. maquina _____ _____

12. Sanchez _____ _____

13. nariz _____ _____

14. ojala _____ _____

15. vendo este _____ _____ (pro)

16. sabado _____ _____

17. profesion _____ _____

18. filosofia _____ _____

19. joven _____ _____

20. Si, quiero _____ _____ (adv/conj)

8

Rule 8

Accents
Rule 9

An accent is placed on a word when it introduces an interrogative or an exclamatory phrase.

(El acento es aplicado en una palabra cuando introduce una pregunta o una exclamación.)

Examples:
1. que   ¿Qué?   (What?)
2. que   ¡Qué!   (What!)

Exercise

Name: _____

Date: _____

Class: _____

These words almost always appear at the beginning of the question. It is very common for these words to appear in a single word question. They require a written accent.

(Casi todo el tiempo, estas palabras aparecen al principio de la pregunta. Es muy común que aparezcan en preguntas de una sóla palabra y requieren un acento escrito.)

These words introduce an interrogative.

Change the following words to questions and apply the accents.
(Cambie las palabras siguientes a preguntas y aplique el acento.)

1. como   ¿Cómo? _____ (How?)
2. cual   _____ (Which?)
3. quien   _____ (Who?)
4. donde   _____ (Where?)
5. cuanto   _____ (How much?)
6. cuando   _____ (When?)
7. cuales   _____ (Which ones?)
8. cuantos   _____ (How many?)
9. ése   _____ (That one?)
10. éste   _____ (This one?)

These words are called palabras Interrogativas

Exercise

Name: _____

Date: _____

Class: _____

These words almost always appear at the beginning of the exclamation. It is very common for these words to appear as single word exclamation. They require a written accent.

(Casi todo el tiempo, estas palabras aparecen al principio de la exclamación. Es muy común que aparezcan en exclamaciones de una sóla palabra y requieren un acento escrito.)

These words are called *palabras Exclamatorias.*

These words introduce an exclamation.

Change the following words to exclamations and apply the accents.
(Cambie las palabras siguientes a exclamaciones y aplique el acento.)

1. como   ¡Có mo! _____ (How!)
2. cual   _____ (Which!)
3. quien   _____ (Who!)
4. donde   _____ (Where!)
5. cuanto   _____ (How much!)
6. cuando   _____ (When!)
7. cuales   _____ (Which ones!)
8. cuantos   _____ (How many!)
9. ése   _____ (That one!)
10. éste   _____ (This one!)

Accents Exercise

Write the following words and add the accent if necessary.

(Escriba las siguientes palabras y escriba el acento si es necesario.)

Name: _____

Date: _____

Class: _____

1. vendio   _____
2. debil   _____
3. gramatica   _____
4. explicacion   _____
5. solo   _____ (adv.)
6. ¿Cuanto?   _____
7. maiz   _____
8. automovil   _____
9. ciudad   _____
10. Atlantico   _____
11. autobus   _____
12. secretaria   _____
13. de   _____ (prep.)
14. ¡Quien!   _____
15. ferrocarril   _____
16. recibi   _____
17. reia   _____
18. comparacion   _____
19. ¿Donde?   _____
20. cuando   _____

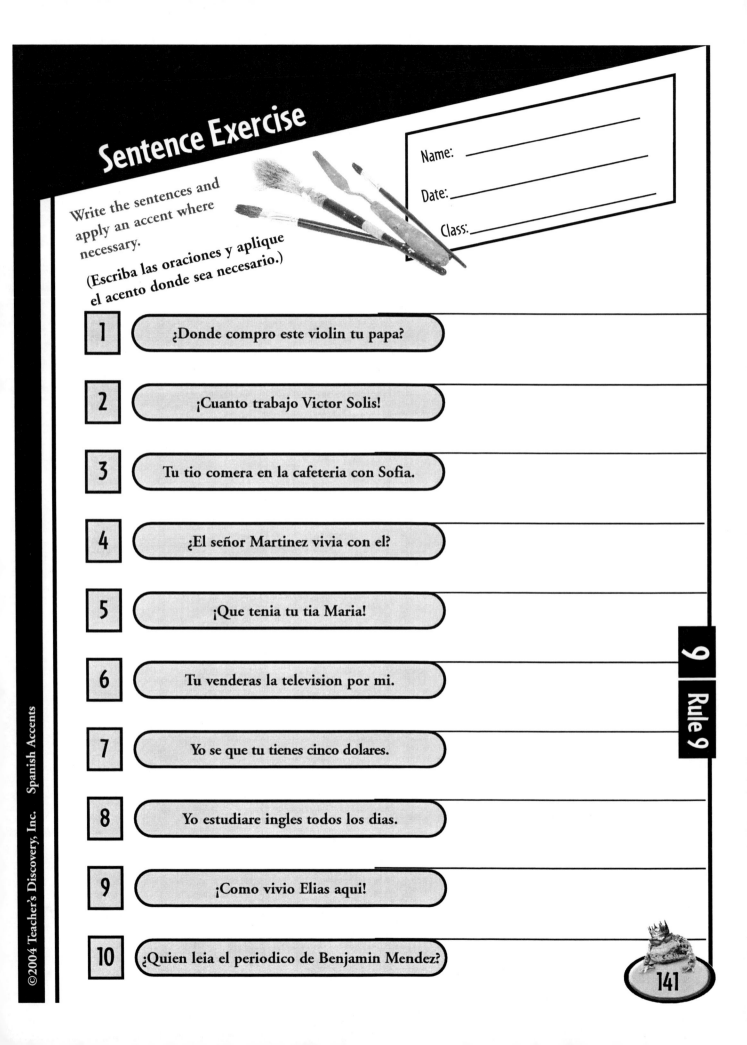

Write the sentences and apply an accent where necessary.

(Escriba las oraciones y aplique el acento donde sea necesario.)

Name: _____

Date: _____

Class: _____

1	¿Donde compro este violin tu papa?
2	¡Cuanto trabajo Victor Solis!
3	Tu tio comera en la cafeteria con Sofia.
4	¿El señor Martinez vivia con el?
5	¡Que tenia tu tia Maria!
6	Tu venderas la television por mi.
7	Yo se que tu tienes cinco dolares.
8	Yo estudiare ingles todos los dias.
9	¡Como vivio Elias aqui!
10	¿Quien leia el periodico de Benjamin Mendez?

9

Rule 9

Add accents if necessary and identify all words as *agudas, graves*, or *esdrújulas*.

(Escriba los acentos si son necesarios e identifique las palabras como agudas, graves o esdrújulas.)

Name: _____
Date: _____
Class: _____

A-Aguda	G-Grave	E-Esdrújula

1. despues _____
2. vivia _____
3. ¿Que? _____
4. examenes _____
5. television _____
6. cancer _____
7. se _____ (verb)
8. tenia _____
9. algodon _____
10. jovenes _____
11. ingles _____
12. ¡Cuando! _____
13. eleccion _____
14. tu _____ (pos. adj.)
15. ¿Quien? _____
16. Juarez _____
17. democrata _____
18. aqui _____
19. inutil _____
20. azul _____

9 | Rule 9

Exercise
Paragraphs with Accents

These paragraphs contain words that do require a written accent.

(Estos párrafos contienen palabras que sí requieren acento escrito.)

Read the paragraphs and apply accents if necessary.

(Lea los párrafos y aplique acentos si son necesarios.)

¿Que tenia tu tia anoche? Hector dijo que ella hablaba de la politica con el capitan Juarez. Tambien dijo que ella es policia y que trabajaba en la carcel. ¿Cuando iras a hablar con ella?

¿Donde viven tus tios? Veronica me dice que antes ellos vivian en America. Ahora viven en Mexico. Alli el tiene un trabajo muy facil en una compañia grande. ¿Cuanto dinero recibira?

9 | Rule 9

143

Test

Name: _____

Date: _____

Class: _____

Write the words, add the accent if necessary, and identify as *agudas*, *graves*, or *esdrujulas*.

(Escriba las palabras, aplique el acento si es necesario e identifique como agudas, graves o esdrujulas.)

A, G or E

Accents

1.	ciudad	_____ _____
2.	hispanico	_____ _____
3.	mi casa	_____ _____ (adj)
4.	util	_____ _____
5.	todavia	_____ _____
6.	leche	_____ _____
7.	condicion	_____ _____
8.	huesped	_____ _____
9.	dijo que si (yes)	_____ _____ (adv)
10.	facil	_____ _____
11.	comeras	_____ _____
12.	azucar	_____ _____
13.	feliz	_____ _____
14.	Elias	_____ _____
15.	¿Donde?	_____ _____
16.	dolares	_____ _____
17.	despues	_____ _____
18.	dificil	_____ _____
19.	platano	_____ _____
20.	¡Cuales!	_____ _____

Rule 9

9

144

Optional Test

Name: _____

Date: _____

Class: _____

Write the words, add the accent if necessary, and identify as *agudas*, *graves* or *esdrujulas*.

Escriba las palabras, aplique el acento si es necesario, e identifique como agudas, graves o esdrújulas.)

A, G or E

Accents

#	Word		
1.	Caracter	_____	_____
2.	mayoria	_____	_____
3.	el libro	_____	_____ (art)
4.	asistia	_____	_____
5.	autobus	_____	_____
6.	director	_____	_____
7.	jardin	_____	_____
8.	carcel	_____	_____
9.	para mi	_____	_____ (pron)
10.	Marquez	_____	_____
11.	religion	_____	_____
12.	dificil	_____	_____
13.	padre	_____	_____
14.	muchos	_____	_____
15.	¿Cuando?	_____	_____
16.	central	_____	_____
17.	numero	_____	_____
18.	recibia	_____	_____
19.	facil	_____	_____
20.	sabado	_____	_____

9 | Rule 9

Accents
Rule 10

Words that combine with object pronouns (direct and indirect object pronouns) and stress the third or fourth syllable from the end of the words require a written accent.

(Las palabras que se combinan con pronombres (pronombres que se usan como objetos directos u objetos indirectos) y tienen el énfasis en la antepenúltima sílaba o en la anterior de la antepenúltima sílaba, requieren un acento escrito.

Examples:
1. háblame   **há** bla me   (Talk to me.)
2. véndeselo   **vén** de se lo   (Sell it to him.)

These words are called *Esdrújulas* or *Sobreesdrújulas*.

Exercise

A single object pronoun (*me, te, se, lo, la, le, nos*, etc.) or a combination of two object pronouns may attach to a word and may cause the stress to be on the 3rd or 4th syllable from the end of the word. In both cases a written accent is required.

These words are called *Esdrújulas* or *Sobreesdrújulas.*

Name: _____

Date: _____

Class: _____

Un pronombre (me, te, se, lo, la, le, nos, etc.) o una combinación de dos pronombres se pueden juntar con una palabra y pueden causar que el énfasis esté en la antepenúltima sílaba o antes de la antepenúltima silaba. En ambos casos se requiere un acento escrito.

Divide the words, circle the stressed syllable, and apply the accent.
(**Divida las palabras, rodee la sílaba con el énfasis y aplique el acento.**

1.	tomalo	(tó) ma lo _____	(Drink it.)
2.	compralos	_____	(Buy them.)
3.	cortala	_____	(Cut it.)
4.	firmalos	_____	(Sign them.)
5.	estudialo	_____	(Study it.)
6.	escribeme	_____	(Write to me.)
7.	llevaselo	_____	(Take it to her.)
8.	cometelo	_____	(You eat it.)
9.	cantaselo	_____	(Sing it for her.)
10.	digamelo	_____	(Tell it to me.)
11.	pideselo	_____	(Ask him for it.)
12.	abreselo	_____	(Open it for him.)

10 | Rule 10

Accents Excercise

Name: _____

Date: _____

Class: _____

Write the following words and add the accent if necessary.

(Escriba las siguientes palabras y escriba el acento si es necesario.)

1. economia _____
2. lider _____
3. cuanto _____
4. aquel _____ (dem. pron.)
5. escribeme _____
6. venderas _____
7. apartamento _____
8. angel _____
9. te _____ (noun)
10. ojala _____
11. digamelo _____
12. examenes _____
13. ¿Ese? _____
14. corria _____
15. joven _____
16. caracter _____
17. solo _____ (adv.)
18. estudialo _____
19. futbol _____
20. llevaselo _____

Sentence Excercise

Write the sentences and apply an accent where necessary.

(Escriba las oraciones y aplique el acento donde sea necesario.)

Name: _____

Date: _____

Class: _____

1 | Tu vendeselo a mi tio por cien dolares. | _____

2 | Hableme por telefono el sabado. | _____

3 | Compralos para Tomas y para mi. | _____

4 | Nicolas y el son medicos en este hospital. | _____

5 | La leccion de ingles es muy dificil. | _____

6 | Tu llevaselo al mecanico el miercoles. | _____

7 | En America hay muchos politicos democratas. | _____

8 | Escribeme la leccion de matematicas aqui. | _____

9 | ¿Cuando seran mis examenes? | _____

10 | Tu pideselo al profesor Cardenas. | _____

10 | Rule 10

149

Paragraphs with Accents

These paragraphs contain words that do require a written accent.

(Estos párrafos contienen palabras que sí requieren un acento escrito.)

Read the paragraphs and apply accents if necessary.

(Lea los párrafos y aplique acentos si son necesarios.)

Mi hermano Hipolito quiere que tu compres cinco lapices. Compralos en ese almacen. Despues llevaselos a su cuarto. Rene quiere un lapiz tambien. Vendeselo por un dolar. ¿Cuando los compraras?

¿Quien vive en este apartamento? Me dicen que dos jovenes. Se llaman Elias y Jose. Ellos pagan cien dolares de renta. Mañana se iran a Panama. A mi me gusta aqui. Hableme por telefono para verlos.

10 | Rule 10

150

Add accents if necessary and identify all words as *agudas, graves, esdrújulas* or *sobreesdrújulas*.

(Escriba los acentos si son necesarios e identifique las palabras como agudas, graves, esdrújulas o sobreesdrújulas.

Name: _____

Date: _____

Class: _____

A-Aguda	G-Grave	E-Esdrújula	S-Sobreesdrújula

1. supervision _____
2. mayoria _____
3. calcetin _____
4. cantasela _____
5. util _____
6. maquina _____
7. plural _____
8. Antonio _____
9. debil _____
10. cometelo _____
11. filosofia _____
12. chocolate _____
13. Davila _____
14. español _____
15. cortala _____
16. Maria _____
17. azucar _____
18. pantalon _____
19. digamelo _____
20. numero _____

Test

Name: _____

Date: _____

Class: _____

Write the words, add the accent if necessary, and identify as *aguda, grave, esdrújula* or *sobreesdrújula.*

(Escriba las palabras, aplique el acento si es necesario, e identifique como agudas, graves, esdrújulas o sobreesdrújulas.

Accents

A, G, E or S

1. amistad _____ _____
2. ¿Donde? _____ _____
3. digamelo _____ _____
4. carretera _____ _____
5. examenes _____ _____
6. escribia _____ _____
7. confesion _____ _____
8. llevaselo _____ _____
9. util _____ _____
10. America _____ _____
11. violin _____ _____
12. tenia _____ _____
13. pideselo _____ _____
14. Francisco _____ _____
15. saludare _____ _____
16. corria _____ _____
17. hablame _____ _____
18. ¡Cuales! _____ _____
19. vendeselo _____ _____
20. adios _____ _____

10 | Rule 10

Accents
Rule 11

Words that join with the suffixes "*mente*" or "*ísimo*" are used as adjectives and adverbs and may require a written accent.

(Las palabras que se juntan con "mente" o "ísimo" se usan como adjetivos o adverbios y podrán requerir acento escrito.)

These words are called *esdrújulas* or *sobreesdrújulas*.

Examples:
1. rapida (rá) pi da men te   (rapidly)
2. fácil (fa) ci lí si mo   (very easy)

11 | Rule 11

Exercise

These words are called *sobreesdrújulas*. Accented words that join with the suffix "*mente*" do not change the spelling, the stress, nor the accent.

(Las palabras que tienen acento y que se juntan con "mente", no cambian la manera de deletrear, ni el énfasis y mantienen el acento.)

Divide the words, circle the stressed syllable, and apply the accent.
(**Divida las palabras, rodee la sílaba con el énfasis y aplique el acento.**

1. facilmente   (fá)cil men te _____ (easily)
2. debilmente   _____ (weakly)
3. historicamente   _____ (historically)
4. politicamente   _____ (politically)
5. dificilmente   _____ (difficulty)
6. matematicamente   _____ (mathematically)
7. tragicamente   _____ (tragically)
8. logicamente   _____ (logically)
9. economicamente   _____ (economically)
10. automaticamente   _____ (automatically)

These words are called *Sobreesdrújulas.*

11 | Rule 11

154

Accents
Rule 11

The suffix "*ísimo, ísima, ísimos,* or *ísimas*", is added to adjectives and occasionally adverbs to obtain the superlative form of the word (very, most, extremely). If the word ends in a consonant, the suffix is added. If the word ends in a vowel, the vowel is dropped to join the suffix.

Name: _____

Date: _____

Class: _____

(El sufijo "*ísimo, ísima, ísimos, o ísimas*"), se agrega a adjetivos y ocasionalmente a adverbios para obtener la forma superlativa de la palabra. Si el adjetivo termina en una consonante, se junta "ísimo". Si termina en vocal, la vocal se quita y se agrega "ísimo" a la palabra.

These words are called *Esdrújulas*.

Divide the words, circle the stressed syllable, and apply the accent.
(Divida las palabras, rodee la sílaba con el énfasis, y aplique el acento.

1. malo   ma (lí) si mo _____ (very bad)
2. azul   _____ (extremely blue)
3. roja   _____ (most red)
4. bueno   _____ (extremely good)
5. débil   _____ (most weak)
6. hermosa   _____ (very beautiful)
7. fuerte   _____ (very strong)
8. grandes   _____ (extremely big)
9. caro   _____ (most expensive)
10. baratas   _____ (very cheap)
11. mucho   _____ (very much)
12. difícil   _____ (most difficult)

11 | Rule 11

Accents Exercise

Write the following words and add the accent if necessary.

(Escriba las siguientes palabras y escriba el acento si es necesario.)

1. ademas _____
2. tomalo _____
3. inteligente _____
4. fuertisimo _____
5. jovenes _____
6. logicamente _____
7. caracter _____
8. cafe _____
9. cometelo _____
10. televisor _____
11. lapiz _____
12. leia _____
13. ¿Cuando? _____
14. feliz _____
15. telefono _____
16. buenisima _____
17. Mendez _____
18. compañia _____
19. politicamente _____
20. ingles _____

Sentence Excercise

Write the sentences and apply an accent where necessary.

(Escriba las oraciones y aplique un acento donde sea necesario.)

Name: _____

Date: _____

Class: _____

1 Victor Ramirez tiene el corazon debilisimo. _____

2 Antes, tu corrias rapidamente. _____

3 Ojala que este carro corra economicamente. _____

4 ¿Cuando compraras este sofa grandisimo? _____

5 Hablame por telefono para ir a la libreria. _____

6 Mi tio Andres murio tragicamente. _____

7 Rene compro este autobus baratisimo. _____

8 Jose vendio su carro facilmente. _____

9 Martin quiere a Maria muchisimo. _____

10 La puerta se abrio automaticamente. _____

Word Identification Exercise

Add accents if necessary and identify all words as *agudas, graves, esdrújulas* or *sobreesdrújulas*.

(Escriba los acentos si son necesarios e identifique las palabras como agudas, graves, esdrújulas o sobreesdrújulas.)

Name: _____

Date: _____

Class: _____

A-Aguda	G-Grave	E-Esdrújula	S-Sobreesdrújula

1. Maria _____
2. ciudad _____
3. firmalos _____
4. ¡Como! _____
5. facilmente _____
6. estudiare _____
7. poblacion _____
8. futbol _____
9. republica _____
10. libreria _____
11. comparacion _____
12. rapidamente _____
13. muchisimo _____
14. luna _____
15. viviran _____
16. dificilmente _____
17. inutil _____
18. Castillon _____
19. hermosisima _____
20. matematicamente _____

Paragraphs with Accents

These paragraphs contain words that do require a written accent.

(Estos párrafos contienen palabras que sí requieren un acento escrito.)

Name: _____

Date: _____

Class: _____

Read the paragraphs and apply accents if necessary.

(Lea los párrafos y aplique acentos si son necesarios.)

Veronica es una muchacha buenisima. Ayer yo comi con ella en un cafe. Alli me ayudo con la leccion de matematicas. Ella la aprendio facilmente. Para mi es muy dificil porque yo no estudio mucho.

Mi tio Cesar es el alcalde de la ciudad. Politicamente, el es un democrata. Mi primo Tobias tambien es un politico. Los dos dicen que la economia de Los Estados Unidos es fuertisima.

11 | Rule 11

159

True or False Test

Is the word correct? True or False!

(¿Está correcta la palabra? ¡Verdad o Falso!

V-Verdad　　　　**F-Falso**

1.	fácil	V	F
2.	jovén	V	F
3.	difícilmente	V	F
4.	córtala	V	F
5.	aleman	V	F
6.	Juárez	V	F
7.	¿este?	V	F
8.	dé (prep.)	V	F
9.	muchísimo	V	F
10.	Miguel	V	F
11.	pajarós	V	F
12.	dírector	V	F
13.	históricamente	V	F
14.	aquél (dem. adj.)	V	F
15.	béisbol	V	F
16.	comételo	V	F
17.	calcetín	V	F
18.	azulisima	V	F
19.	té (noun)	V	F
20.	opinión	V	F

Test

Write the words, add the accent if necessary, and identify as *aguda, grave, esdrújula,* or *sobreesdrújula.*

(Escriba las palabras, aplique el acento si es necesario e identifique como agudas, graves, esdrújulas o sobreesdrújulas.)

Accents

A, G, E or S

1. estudialo _____ _____
2. ¿Cuales? _____ _____
3. Concepcion _____ _____
4. digamelo _____ _____
5. Javier _____ _____
6. examenes _____ _____
7. facilisimo _____ _____
8. niños _____ _____
9. corazon _____ _____
10. automatica _____ _____
11. debilmente _____ _____
12. frances _____ _____
13. arbol _____ _____
14. cantasela _____ _____
15. cafe _____ _____
16. simpatico _____ _____
17. dificilmente _____ _____
18. ¡Como! _____ _____
19. Castillon _____ _____
20. mecanico _____ _____

Optional Test

Write the words, add the accent if necessary, and identify as *agudas*, *graves*, *esdrújulas*, or *sobreesdrújulas*.

(Escriba las palabras, aplique el acento si es necesario, e identifique como agudas, graves, esdrújulas, o sobreesdrújulas.)

A, G, E or S

Accents

1. compralos _____ _____
2. ¡Que! _____ _____
3. aprenderia _____ _____
4. facilmente _____ _____
5. Arturo _____ _____
6. miercoles _____ _____
7. muchisimo _____ _____
8. television _____ _____
9. despues _____ _____
10. pideselo _____ _____
11. lapices _____ _____
12. joven _____ _____
13. ¿Cuantos? _____ _____
14. compramelas _____ _____
15. azulisimo _____ _____
16. dolares _____ _____

11 | Rule 11

Answer Key

Accents

- *Spanish accents workbook*
- *This workbook covers 11 rules and*
- *Contains 144 exercises for classroom use*

Written by
José R. Moreno

Page 19

1. **me** sa
2. **hi** jo
3. **ga** to
4. **ro** jo
5. **ni** ño
6. **no** ta
7. **ma** lo
8. **hi** ja
9. **to** ro
10. **ri** co
11. **al** to
12. **sa** la
13. **bo** ca
14. **lu** na
15. **ba** ño

Page 20

1. **ca** lle
2. **pe** rro
3. **si** lla
4. **le** che
5. **pa** dre
6. **li** bro
7. **mu** cho
8. **lu** nes
9. **jo** ven
10. **car** ta
11. **plu** mas
12. **dul** ce
13. **flo** res
14. **nue** vo
15. **tien** da

Page 21

1. **A** na
2. **Ro** sa
3. **Ri** ta
4. **Ed** na
5. **Ol** ga
6. **Do** ra
7. **Car** los
8. **Ma** rio
9. **Pe** dro
10. **Dia** na
11. **Pa** blo
12. **Ir** ma
13. **Ju** lio
14. **Blan** ca
15. **Car** men

Page 22

1. **dul** ces
2. **ro** jo
3. **li** bro
4. **tien** da
5. **jo** ven
6. **lu** nes
7. **me** sa
8. **car** ta
9. **Pe** dro
10. **ca** lle
11. **al** to
12. **Car** men
13. **mu** chos
14. **A** na
15. **nue** vos
16. **sa** la
17. **le** che
18. **Di** ana
19. **to** ro
20. **Ma** rio

Page 23

1. **Do**ra y **Pe**dro **ha**blan con el **jo**ven.
2. **Ju**lio es **hi**jo de **Blan**ca.
3. La **tien**da **nue**va **ven**de pan, **le**che y **dul**ces.
4. A mi **pa**dre le **gus**ta el **li**bro de **Car**men.
5. En la **ca**sa **ten** go **u**na **me**sa con **cin**co **si**llas.
6. El **ga**to **ne**gro de Mario es **ma**lo.
7. **Ri**ta y **Pa**blo **tie**nen un **ca**rro **ro**jo.
8. El **to**ro **gran**de **co**rre **mu**cho.
9. **Ir**ma **tie**ne **mu**chas **flo**res en la **sa**la.
10. La **hi**ja de **Ed**na es **al**ta y **jo**ven.

Page 24

Yo soy **pa**dre de tres **hi**jos. **To**dos son **ri**cos. Mi **hi**jo se **lla**ma **Car**los. Es un **jo** ven **bue**no y muy **al**to que **vi**ve en **u**na **ca**sa **chi**ca. Su **ni** ño **tie**ne un **pe**rro muy **gran**de y un **ga**to muy **ma**lo. Mis **hi**jas se **lla**man **Ol**ga y **Dia**na. Ellas **tie**nen **u**na **ca**sa **nue**va y en la **sa**la **tie**nen **u**na **me**sa **ro**ja con **mu**chas **si**llas. Ellas **vi**ven **cer**ca de mi **ca**sa. **Dia** na **tie**ne un **ca**rro **nue**vo. **Siem**pre **vie**nen a mi **ca**sa los **lu**nes.

Page 25
1. bo **ni** ta
2. ma **ña** na
3. di **ne** ro
4. a **mi** go
5. za **pa** to
6. pi **za** rra
7. pe **lo** ta
8. her **ma** no
9. co **mi** da
10. fa **mi** lia
11. pa **pe** les
12. her **mo** sa

Page 26
1. se **ño** ri ta
2. ca rre **te** ra
3. es cri **to** rio
4. pre si **den** te
5. cho co **la** te
6. me xi **ca** no
7. se cre **ta** ria
8. a me ri **ca** no
9. a par ta **men** to
10. in te li **gen** te

Page 27
1. Ro **ber** to
2. Fe **li** pe
3. Ri **car** do
4. E **duar** do
5. An **to** nio
6. Pa **tri** cia
7. Le **ti** cia
8. Gra **cie** la
9. Ar **man** do
10. Es **te** ban
11. Fran **cis** co
12. Jo se **fi** na
13. Gua da **lu** pe
14. E van ge **li** na
15. Ma xi mi **lia** no

Page 28
1. se cre **ta** rias
2. **plu** mas
3. fa **mi** lia
4. **ca** lle
5. **Dia** na
6. pi **za** rra
7. a par ta **men** to
8. her **mo** sa
9. **ni** ño
10. a me ri **ca** no
11. **pe** rros
12. **tien** das
13. pa **pe** les
14. pre si **den** te
15. bo **ni** tas
16. **mu** cha
17. es cri **to** rios
18. **car** ta
19. ca rre **te** ra
20. a **mi** go

Page 29
1. Mi **a**migo **tie**ne **mu**cho di**ne**ro.
2. **E**duar**do** **com**pra comi**da** y **flo**res.
3. El presi**den**te **vi**ve con su fa**mi**lia.
4. **La** secretaria **ven**de los chocola**tes** mexi**ca**nos.
5. Mario estudia en su escri**to**rio.
6. Mi her**ma**no es **jo**ven y **al**to.
7. Josefina **ha**bla **mu**cho con Pa**tri**cia.
8. Mi **pa**dre **tie**ne **u**na **tien**da de za**pa**tos.
9. El mucha**cho** **co**rre por la **ca**lle.
10. Pedro bebe **mu**cha **le**che.

Page 30
Mi **pa**dre Fran**cis**co **tie**ne un her**ma**no que **tie**ne **u**na **tien**da de comi**da**. Su **nom**bre es Ri**car**do y es el presi**den**te die su ne**go**cio. Ri**car**do es muy inteli**gen**te y **vi**ve en un aparta**men**to **gran**de con su fa**mi**lia. Su es**po**sa Guada**lu**pe es muy boni**ta** y es su secre**ta**ria. Sus **hi**jas **Dia**na y Pa**tri**cia son estu**dian**tes y a**sis**ten al colegio. **E**llas **es**tudian **pa**ra ser profe**so**ras y en las **no**ches traba**jan** en la **tien**da.

Page 31

1. me xi **ca** no
2. pe **lo** ta
3. **mu** chos
4. **Car** men
5. her **ma** no
6. **li** bro
7. di **ne** ro
8. **nue** vo
9. bo **ni** to
10. E van ge **li** na
11. za **pa** tos
12. **le** che
13. **Pe** dro
14. in te li **gen** te
15. ma **ña** na
16. se ño **ri** ta
17. **si** lla
18. cho co **la** te
19. Gua da **lu** pe
20. **flo** res

Page 34

1. pa **pel**
2. mu **jer**
3. plu **ral**
4. fe **liz**
5. ciu **dad**
6. ho **tel**
7. a **yer**
8. re **loj**
9. lo **cal**
10. mo **tor**
11. cen **tral**
12. sa **lud**
13. doc **tor**
14. se **ñor**
15. na **riz**

Page 35

1. A **bel**
2. E **loy**
3. Fi **del**
4. O **mar**
5. I **nés**
6. Da **vid**
7. Vi **dal**
8. Fe **liz**
9. Da **niel**
10. Ra **quel**
11. Ga **briel**
12. Ma **nuel**
13. Or **tiz**
14. Sa **muel**
15. Mi **guel**

Page 36

1. us **ted**
2. **lu** ne
3. **ha** blan
4. doc **tor**
5. **Ju** lio
6. a **rroz**
7. Da **vid**
8. **jo** ven
9. plu **ral**
10. **hi** jos
11. ciu **dad**
12. mu **jer**
13. sa **lud**
14. **dul** ce
15. Fi **del**
16. re **loj**
17. **co** men
18. a **yer**
19. a **zul**
20. **Car** men

Page 37

1. **Fe**lix **ha**bla con el **jo**ven en el ho**tel**.
2. **A**yer Pa**tri**cia y Ra**quel** ha**bla** ban con el doc**tor**.
3. El **ca**rro de Da**niel** es co**lor** a**zul**.
4. En **e**sa **tien**da se**ven**den pa**pel** y **plu**mas.
5. En la ciu**dad** de San An**to**nio **vi**ve Ma**nuel** Or**tiz**.
6. El re**loj** **nue**vo de Mi**guel** se**ven**de por **mu**cho di**ne**ro.
7. **E**sa mu**jer** **al**ta se **lla**ma I**nés** Ba**rrien**tos.
8. La **tro**ca de Vi**dal** **tie**ne un mo**tor** **gran**de.
9. La ofi**ci**na cen**tral** **tie**ne un departa**men**to de sa**lud**.
10. El a**mi**go de Ga**briel** **tie**ne la na**riz** que**bra**da.

Page 39

Fran**cis**co **ha**bla con Mi**guel** en su aparta**men**to. **Quie**re com**prar** un **ca**rro a**zul**. **A**yer ha**bla**ba con el **due**ño del **ca**rro. Se **lla**ma Da**niel** Or**tiz** y **vi**ve en la ciu**dad** de La**re**do. Es doc**tor** y **tie**ne su ofi**ci**na en un ho**tel** **cer**ca de la carre**te**ra. Mi secre**ta**ria Ra**quel** lo co**no**ce. **Di**ce que **vi**ve muy fe**liz** con su mu**jer** y con sus dos **hi**jos **A**bel y **O**mar. **Tie**nen el **ca**rro en un lo**cal** de **ven**ta.

Accents - Answer Sheet

P. 45 is on the next Answer Sheet

Page 38
1. G
2. A
3. A
4. G
5. G
6. A
7. G
8. A
9. A
10. G
11. G
12. A
13. A
14. G
15. A
16. G
17. G
18. A
19. G
20. A

Page 40
1. **al** tos — G
2. Ga **briel** — A
3. pi **za** rra — G
4. doc **tor** — A
5. pre si **den** te — G
6. a **zul** — A
7. se **ñor** — A
8. Da **vid** — A
9. **ca** lles — G
10. **plu** ma — G
11. na **riz** — A
12. Ri **car** do — G
13. Sando **val** — A
14. **pa** dre — G
15. mu **jer** — A
16. Gra **cie** la — G
17. a me ri **ca** no — G
18. ciu **dad** — A
19. Or **tiz** — A
20. **tien** da — G

Page 41
1. ge ne **ral**
2. re gu **lar**
3. Na vi **dad**
4. sin gu **lar**
5. es pa **ñol**
6. pro fe **sor**
7. ca pi **tal**
8. li ber **tad**
9. su pe **rior**
10. na cio **nal**
11. a mis **tad**
12. di rec **tor**

Page 42
1. cal cu la **dor**
2. re si den **cial**
3. fe rro ca **rril**
4. te le vi **sor**
5. di fi cul **tad**
6. hu ma ni **dad**
7. fe li ci **dad**
8. en fer me **dad**
9. u ni ver si **dad**
10. ad mi nis tra **dor**
11. in ves ti ga **dor**
12. per so na li **dad**

Page 43
1. Ja **vier**
2. I sa **bel**
3. Ra fa **el**
4. Is ra **el**
5. A ma **dor**
6. Es co **bar**
7. Sal va **dor**
8. Ma ri **sol**
9. Is ma **el**
10. A gui **lar**
11. San do **val**
12. Es qui **vel**
13. Ve ra **cruz**
14. A po li **nar**
15. Vi lla rre **al**

Page 44
1. a mis **tad**
2. pa **pe** les
3. na **riz**
4. re gu **lar**
5. pre si **den** te
6. di fi cul **tad**
7. doc **to** res
8. Es qui **vel**
9. **ca** lles
10. hos pi **tal**
11. in ves ti ga **dor**
12. na cio **nal**
13. Ve ra **cruz**
14. se ño **ri** tas
15. fe li ci **dad**
16. **mu** chos
17. fe rro ca **rril**
18. A gui **lar**
19. za **pa** tos
20. E **duar** do

Page 46
1. A
2. G
3. G
4. A
5. G
6. A
7. A
8. G
9. G
10. A
11. A
12. A
13. G
14. A
15. G
16. A
17. A
18. G
19. G
20. A

167

Page 45

1. El administra**dor** es herm**a**no de Ma**nuel** Villarre**al**.
2. Mi **pa**dre escri**be car**tas en espa**ñol**.
3. El direc**tor** del **cen**tro de sa**lud** es Ja**vier**.
4. **Car**los y Ama**dor tie**nen muy **bue**na amis**tad**.
5. Isra**el** es profe**sor** en la universi**dad**.
6. El se**ñor** Ri**car**do **su**fre de **u**na enferme**dad ma**la.
7. El ferroca**rril pa**sa por la capi**tal** naci**o**nal.
8. El **jo**ven es muy fe**liz** con su **no**via.
9. El presi**den**te **tie**ne **u**na personali**dad** muy bo**ni**ta.
10. La señori**ta Dia**na tra**ba**ja en el hospi**tal** gene**ral**.

Page 47

El **pa**dre de Mari**sol** se **lla**ma **Pe**dro Esco**bar**. Tra**ba**ja en la ciu**dad** de El **Pa**so en el Departa**men**to de Sa**lud**. **Tie**ne muy **bue**na amis**tad** con el doc**tor por** que **ha**bla espa**ñol** muy bien.

La secre**ta**ria del administra**dor** de la universi**dad** se **lla**ma **Ol**ga Sando**val**. **E**lla es **u**na mu**jer** muy inteli**gen**te **pe**ro **tie**ne dificul**tad** con el espa**ñol**. A**yer e**lla habla**ba** con el profe**sor** Agui**lar**.

Page 48

1. me xi **ca** no	G
2. li ber **tad**	A
3. a **mi** gos	G
4. Fran **cis** co	G
5. re **loj**	A
6. na cio **nal**	A
7. fe **liz**	A
8. co **mi** da	G
9. I sa **bel**	A
10. **jo** ven	G
11. re si den **cial**	A
12. a **yer**	A
13. **Dia** na	G
14. es cri **to** rios	G
15. a mis **tad**	A
16. ca rre **te** ras	G
17. **ro** jo	G
18. per so na li **dad**	A
19. Ma **nuel**	A
20. **Car** men	G

Page 50

1. pa **pá**
2. vio **lín**
3. a **diós**
4. mi **llón**
5. a **quí**
6. jar **dín**
7. so **fá**
8. fran **cés**
9. a **llí**
10. des **pués**
11. tam **bién**
12. ca **fé**

Page 51

1. ha **blé**
2. co **mí**
3. vi **vió**
4. a **brí**
5. ven **dió**
6. be **bí**
7. com **pró**
8. i **ré**
9. ve **rás**
10. se **rán**
11. en **tr**
12. da **ré**

Page 52

1. José
2. Martín
3. Jesús
4. Rubén
5. Ramón
6. Tomás
7. Andrés
8. René
9. Adrián
10. Cantú
11. Inés
12. Galván
13. Solís
14. Chacón
15. Román

Page 53

1. **dul** ces
2. fran **cés**
3. ciu **dad**
4. a **quí**
5. **flo** res
6. fe li ci **dad**
7. I sa **bel**
8. a **diós**
9. So **lís**
10. fe **liz**
11. **Car** men
12. tam **bién**
13. cen **tral**
14. des **pués**
15. vio **lín**
16. i **ré**
17. **pa** dre
18. pro fe **sor**
19. jar **dín**
20. Es **te** ban

Page 55

1.	tiendas	G
2.	vendió	A
3.	Jesús	A
4.	Apolinar	A
5.	Mario	G
6.	después	A
7.	humanidad	A
8.	familia	G
9.	feliz	A
10.	lunes	G
11.	chacón	A
12.	Antonio	G
13.	adiós	A
14.	Esquirel	A
15.	universidad	A
16.	vivió	A
17.	singular	A
18.	hablan	G
19.	también	A
20.	reloj	A

Page 57

1.	nuevos	G
2.	Carlos	G
3.	Chacón	A
4.	padre	G
5.	francés	A
6.	escritorio	G
7.	Andrés	A
8.	joven	G
9.	después	A
10.	amistad	A
11.	tiendas	G
12.	personalidad	A
13.	aquí	A
14.	feliz	A
15.	superior	A
16.	adiós	A
17.	secretaria	G
18.	violín	A
19.	carreteras	G
20.	Galván	A

Page 54

1. Martín vivió en este hotel con su mamá.
2. A mi papá le gusta tomar café después de comer.
3. Andrés y Carlos serán doctores también.
4. Román compró un reloj por un millón de pesos.
5. Salvador Galván es un joven muy feliz.
6. José le vendió su violín nuevo a Amador.
7. Marisol Cantú comió con Tomás aquí.
8. Allí yo hablé con el profesor de inglés.
9. Ramón le dijo adiós a Inés en el jardín.
10. Yo no le daré ese sofá a Adrián.

Page 56

La mamá de Rubén se llama Blanca. Ella vivió en San Antonio con su hermano René. Allí ella habló puro inglés y nade de español. Yo también iré a esa ciudad, pero yo quiero aprender francés.

José vendió su carro. Hace dos años lo compró por un millón de pesos. Mi papá insiste que compre la camioneta de Tomás y que también compre el violín de Ramón. Mañana iré con ellos a comprar las dos cosas.

Page 58

1. ja po nés
2. a le mán
3. co ra zón
4. al go dón
5. o ja lá
6. calce tín
7. al ma cén
8. pan ta lón
9. cin tu rón
10. a de más
11. ma ti né
12. bai la rín

Page 59

1. ha bla **ré**
2. es cri **bí**
3. co me **rás**
4. vi vi **rán**
5. com pra **ré**
6. tra ba **jó**
7. a bri **rá**
8. ven de **rás**
9. re ci **bí**
10. es tu dia **rás**
11. sa lu da **ré**
12. ca mi na **rán**

Page 61

1. Du rán
2. Guz mán
3. Fe lán
4. Pa na má
5. Jo a quín
6. Cal de rón
7. A gus tín
8. Ni co lás
9. A le mán
10. Ben ja mín
11. Cas ti llón
12. A lar cón
13. Yu ca tán
14. O bre gón
15. Mi cho a cán

Page 62

1. in **glés**
2. en fer me **dad**
3. es cri **bí**
4. **jo** ven
5. ca pi **tán**
6. ge ne **ral**
7. Ni co **lás**
8. **plu** mas
9. a **diós**
10. au to **bús**
11. se cre **ta** rias
12. Ve ra **cruz**
13. ca mi na **rán**
14. ja po **nés**
15. te le vi **sor**
16. co ra **zón**
17. pi **za** rra
18. A le **mán**
19. fe li ci **dad**
20. o ja **lá**

Page 62

1. Benjamín compró una camisa de algodón.
2. El señor Guzmán abrirá la tienda también.
3. Ojalá que mi hermano Agustín venga en autobús.
4. Ese japonés no vivió en Panamá.
5. David y Jesús caminarán con mi papa.
6. Allí mi mamá comerá en un café francés.
7. Aquí yo saludaré al capitán Escobar.
8. Ese japonés vendió el reloj ayer.
9. Martín y Adrián comerán en la universidad.
10. Después yo hablaré con el profesor Calderón.

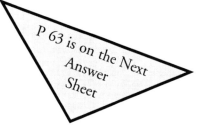

P 63 is on the Next Answer Sheet

Page 64

El profesor Alarcón enseña español y francés en la universidad. Allí asisten Inés y José. Ellos estudian inglés. Yo estudiaré español. Mañana yo iré a hablar con el director Cantú.

Mi hermano Rubén trabaja en un almacén. Allí tiene que saber inglés y también tiene que usar una camisa y un pantalón azul. El dueño es japonés y vivió en Yucatán. Ojalá sean amigos.

Page 63

1. sillas — G
2. recibí — A
3. jardín — A
4. nariz — A
5. serán — A
6. calcetín — A
7. nacional — A
8. Michoacán — A
9. estudiarás — A
10. papeles — G
11. pantalón — A
12. superior — A
13. Andrés — A
14. padres — G
15. Yucatán — A
16. violín — A
17. Ortiz — A
18. mexicana — G
19. almacén — A
20. Leticia — G

Page 65

1. nacional — A
2. bailarín — A
3. familia — G
4. vendió — A
5. estudiaré — A
6. Gabriel — A
7. ojalá — A
8. calculador — A
9. Diana — G
10. Castillón — A
11. Veracruz — A
12. corazón — A
13. apartamentos — G
14. jardín — A
15. Adrián — A
16. central — A
17. vivirán — A
18. felicidad — A
19. Nicolás — A
20. Isabel — A

Page 67

1. **dó** lar
2. **ár** bol
3. **án** gel
4. **ú** til
5. **hués** ped
6. **cár** cel
7. **lí** der
8. **dé** bil
9. **sué** ter
10. **cán** cer
11. **fút** bol
12. **béis** bol

Page 68

1. Durán — A
2. recibí — A
3. hermosa — G
4. violín — A
5. naris — G
6. tambíen — A
7. libertad — A
8. millon — A
9. bonitas — G
10. joven — G
11. autobus — A
12. calles — G
13. pantalón — A
14. natural — A
15. Panamá — A
16. calcetín — A
17. ciudad — A
18. pluma — G
19. algodon — A
20. mujer — A

P 70 & 72 are on the next Answer Sheet

Page 71

1. Ayer yo escribí con mi lápiz.
2. Andrés compró un suéter por un dólar.
3. Joaquín le dijo adiós a Inés.
4. El capitán Vásquez venderá su mesa grande.
5. Mi papá abrirá la puerta del autobús.
6. Javier y Héctor caminarán por aquí hoy.
7. La salud del señor Sánchez es muy débil.
8. Víctor hablaba con el líder en el jardín.
9. César estaba en la cárcel de la ciudad.
10. Es muy fácil comprar este sofá francés.

Page 73

Aquí trabaja el profesor César López. Su esposa Olga es profesora también. Ellos enseñan francés y alemán. Ellos dicen que después quieren ir a vivir a San Francisco. Allí vivirán con la mamá de ella.

Ayer yo hablé con el papá de Rubén. Me dijo que la semana pasada vendió unos zapatos color café. También me dijo que con ese dinero compró un pantalón de algodón y un cinturón muy bonito.

Page 69
1. Gó mez
2. Ló pez
3. Pé rez
4. Ce sar
5. Héc tor
6. Víc tor
7. Chá vez
8. Juá rez
9. Sán chez
10. Mén dez
11. Vás quez
12. Ná ñez
13. Vé lez
14. Már quez
15. Mú niz

Page 70
1. fa **mi** lias
2. **án** gel
3. plu **ral**
4. al go **dón**
5. **plu** mas
6. Jo se **fi** na
7. al ma **cén**
8. in te li **gen** te
9. **cár** cel
10. na **riz**
11. jar **dín**
12. li ber **tad**
13. **hués** ped
14. mu **jer**
15. Ma ri **sol**
16. **sué** ter
17. A gus **tín**
18. **fút** bol
19. di rec **tor**
20. **Mén** dez

Page 72
1. corazón
2. inteligentes
3. béisbol
4. ciudad
5. Esquivel
6. huésped
7. Adrián
8. universida
9. árbol
10. reloj
11. Evangelina
12. algodón
13. Juárez
14. secretaria
15. Ortiz
16. compraré
17. Carlos
18. útil
19. Eduardo
20. ferrocarril

A G G A A G A A G A G A G A G G A A G G A

Page 74
1. almacén
2. Antonio
3. árbol
4. hospital
5. comerás
6. Benjamín
7. joven
8. Samuel
9. Pérez
10. calcetín
11. cáncer
12. Esteban
13. superior
14. Méndez
15. Yucatán
16. americanos
17. fútbol
18. Guadalupe
19. autobús
20. huésped

A G G A A G A A G A G A G A G G A A G G A G

Page 76
1. Suá rez
2. Nú ñez
3. Ra mí rez
4. Ji mé nez
5. I bá ñez
6. Cris tó bal
7. Her nán dez
8. Ro drí guez
9. Mar tí nez
10. Ve lás quez
11. Fer nán dez
12. Gon zá lez
13. Do mín guez
14. Gu tié rrez
15. Me lén drez

Page 77
1. ca pi **tán**
2. en fer me **dad**
3. ca **rác** ter
4. ven **dió**
5. cen **tral**
6. Fer **nán** dez
7. a le **mán**
8. ad mi nis tra **dor**
9. **cár** cel
10. au to **bús**
11. An **drés**
12. **Án** gel
13. **jo** ven
14. Mar **tí** nez
15. es cri **to** rio
16. a **zú** car
17. es cri **bí**
18. na **riz**
19. **Chá** vez
20. Da **vid**

Page 79
1. estéril   G
2. capital   A
3. útil   G
4. cáncer   G
5. Leticia   G
6. después   A
7. Gutiérrez   G
8. feliz   A
9. bailarín   A
10. Maximiliano   G
11. fácil   G
12. Calderón   A
13. abrí   A
14. algodón   A
15. Vásquez   G
16. libertad   A
17. Antonio   G
18. inmóvil   G
19. López   G
20. Castillón   A

Page 75
1. a **zú** car
2. di **fí** cil
3. ca **rác** ter
4. i **nú** til
5. es **té** ril
6. in **mó** vil
7. re **vól** ver
8. ca **dá** ver
9. in **há** bil
10. au to **mó** vil

P 78 is on the next Answer Sheet

172

Accents - Answer Sheet

Page 78

1. La tienda de Omar González vendió todo el azúcar.
2. El capitán compró un revólver alemán.
3. Mi hermano Víctor juega béisbol y fútbol.
4. El líder francés no habla inglés ni español.
5. Raquel Ramírez limpia su automóvil nuevo.
6. Es muy difícil tener un jardín con muchas flores.
7. Su mamá tiene el corazón muy débil.
8. Ese huésped japonés tiene un carácter muy bueno.
9. El viaje de Jesús a Panamá es inútil.
10. Martín Rodríguez escribe con lápiz también.

Page 80

José trabaja aquí. Vende camisas de algodón. Es muy difícil el trabajo porque el dueño es japonés. Yo trabajo con René Domínguez. Nosotros vendemos un millón de pantalones cada año. Ojalá también vendamos muchas camisas.

Mi amigo Cristóbal vive por la calle Obregón. Es fácil llegar a su casa. Vive cerca de la cárcel. Allí vive con su mamá y tienen un automóvil nuevo. También tienen un jardín con un árbol muy grande.

Page 81

1. F
2. V
3. F
4. V
5. V
6. F
7. F
8. F
9. V
10. V
11. V
12. V
13. V
14. F
15. V
16. F
17. F
18. V
19. V
20. F

Page 82

1. Javier — A
2. Joaquín — A
3. universidad — A
4. béisbol — G
5. Eduardo — G
6. después — A
7. cadáver — G
8. violín — A
9. compraré — A
10. dificultad — A
11. Suárez — G
12. feliz — A
13. Nicolás — A
14. superior — A
15. ferrocarril — A
16. Fernández — G
17. Francisco — G
18. dólar — G
19. Adrián — A
20. Sánchez — G

Page 83

1. Jiménez — G
2. azúcar — G
3. francés — A
4. López — G
5. pesos — G
6. ángel — G
7. Salvador — A
8. vendió — A
9. cárcel — G
10. jardín — A
11. difícil — G
12. Ramón — A
13. azul — A
14. Julio — G
15. débil — G
16. Martínez — G
17. Marisol — A
18. allí — A
19. huésped — G
20. japonés — A

Page 85

1. **pá** jar o
2. **mé** di co
3. **mú** si ca
4. **nú** me ro
5. **plá** ta no
6. **sá** ba do
7. **fá** ci les
8. **sí** la ba
9. **má** qui na
10. **jó** ve nes
11. **miér** co les
12. **dó** la res

Page 86

1. **Mó** ni ca
2. **Mé** xi co
3. **Dá** vi la
4. **Cár** de nas
5. **Mé** ri da
6. **Cór** do va
7. **Pán** fi lo
8. **Cá** sa res
9. **Né** li da
10. **Cán** di do

Page 88

1. Irma Cásares compró este sofá por veinte dólares.
2. Yo no estudiaré música en la universidad.
3. La mamá de Jesús abrirá la oficina el sábado.
4. El capitán se llama Héctor Dávila.
5. Los jóvenes juegan béisbol en México.
6. César es huésped en la casa del médico.
7. En el jardín estaba el pájaro de Joaquín.
8. Cándido trabaja con la máquina número tres.
9. Ramón y Nélida venderán plumas y lápices.
10. El líder estaba en la cárcel también.

Page 90

Este miércoles Patricia comerá en un café. Después irá a su hotel. Vive en el cuarto número dos. Allí verá a su novio Héctor. Es profesor de ciencia en la Universidad de México.

Ojalá que los jóvenes compren la máquina de escribir. La vendo por veinte dólares. Con ella yo escribí reportes muy difíciles en la clase de inglés. Mañana le compraré otra a Nicolás Cárdenas.

Page 87

1. sal **ud**
2. cho co **la** te
3. **má** qui na
4. pi **za** rra
5. i **nú** til
6. cas ti **llón**
7. **lí** der
8. Ar **man** do
9. a de **más**
10. **jo** ven
11. fe li ci **dad**
12. **miér** coles
13. a bri **rá**
14. **án** gel
15. **si** llas
16. **Mó** ni ca
17. na **riz**
18. cin tu **rón**
19. **ár** bol
20. ho **tel**

Page 89

1. Fidel — A
2. Méndez — G
3. sílaba — E
4. Andrés — A
5. lápiz — G
6. Evangelina — G
7. adiós — A
8. plátan — E
9. pizarra — G
10. saludaré — A
11. fáciles — E
12. Sandoval — A
13. béisbol — G
14. Mérida — E
15. amigos — G
16. vivirán — A
17. suéter — G
18. Galván — A
19. Graciela — G
20. dólares — E

Page 91

1. autobús — A
2. pájaros — E
3. enfermedad — A
4. cáncer — G
5. hermanos — G
6. capitán — A
7. máquina — E
8. líder — G
9. superior — A
10. Alarcón — A
11. miércoles — E
12. Francisco — G
13. pantalón — A
14. número — E
15. Jiménez — G
16. Raquel — A
17. dólar — G
18. abrirá — A
19. Márquez — G
20. feliz — A

Page 92

1. me **cá** ni co
2. po **lí** ti ca
3. his **pá** ni co
4. e **xá** me nes
5. pe **rió** di co
6. ca **tó** li co
7. his **tó** ri co
8. gra **má** ti ca
9. re **pú** bli ca
10. de **mó** cra ta
11. sim **pá** ti co
12. ma te **má** ti ca

Page 93
1. A **mé** ri ca
2. Ve **ró** ni ca
3. E **rén** di da
4. Se **púl** ve da
5. Que **ré** ta ro
6. Ge **ró** ni mo
7. Hi **pó** li to
8. An **gé** li ca
9. Pa **cí** fi co
10. A **tlán** ti co

Page 94
1. **Ós** car
2. **Á** fri ca
3. **Á** vi la
4. **Án** gel
5. **Án** ge les
6. **Án** gu lo
7. Ál va rez
8. I **ñí** guez
9. **Á** gui la
10. **Á** va los

Page 95
1. cartas
2. estéril
3. matemática
4. ferrocarril
5. jardín
6. joven
7. Pacífico
8. carácter
9. vivirán
10. pizarra
11. Velásquez
12. residencial
13. católico
14. cárcel
15. Carmen
16. algodón
17. automóvil
18. pájaro
19. enfermedad
20. Tomás

Page 97
1. nacional — A
2. hispánico — E
3. presidente — G
4. jardín — A
5. suéter — G
6. plátano — E
7. Cristóbal — G
8. calculador — A
9. papeles — G
10. Esquivel — A
11. azúcar — G
12. Angélica — E
13. libertad — A
14. inteligente — G
15. matemática — E
16. comí — A
17. estéril — G
18. automático — E
19. central — A
20. Atlántico — E

Page 96
1. El mecánico compró un carro por cien dólares.
2. Óscar es el líder de los demócratas.
3. Yo escribí los exámenes fáciles.
4. El periódico americano es de Verónica Múzquiz.
5. La gramática del inglés no es fácil.
6. José González vivió cerca del Pacífico.
7. La República de México tiene una carretera histórica.
8. El joven simpático habló por teléfono.
9. Mi hermano Ramón juega béisbol en Querétaro.
10. Los jóvenes católicos no son políticos.

Page 98
El señor Fernández es un demócrata. El sábado tiene una junta política. Allí hablan por teléfono con representantes de la República de México. El capitán Dávila es el presidente del grupo.

El carro de Andrés es automático. Lo compró nuevo por cinco mil dólares. Mi hermano Agustín es mecánico y dice que el carro es bueno. Mi mamá quiere comprar uno también. El miércoles irá a ver uno.

Page 99

1.	sílaba	E
2.	residencial	A
3.	Suárez	G
4.	Cachón	A
5.	calles	G
6.	mecánico	E
7.	compraré	A
8.	Antonio	G
9.	líder	G
10.	plural	A
11.	inútil	G
12.	gramática	E
13.	Chávez	G
14.	español	A
15.	señoritas	G
16.	América	E
17.	ojalá	A
F 18.	azúcar	G
19.	amistad	A
20	simpático	E

Page 101

1.	lec **ción**	
2.	a **vión**	
3.	re gión	
4.	u **nión**	
5.	can **ción**	
6.	mi **sión**	
7.	ac **ción**	
8.	pa **sión**	
9.	pen **sión**	
10.	men **ción**	
11.	man **sión**	
12.	lo **ción**	

Page 102

1.	ciudad
2.	misión
3.	difícil
4.	México
5.	histórico
6.	loción
7.	administrador
8.	inútil
9.	escribí
10.	González
11.	inglés
12.	hijos
13.	almacén
14.	acción
15.	exámenes
16.	familias
17.	Atlántico
18.	Pérez
19.	abrirá
20.	humanidad

Page 104

1.	escritorio	G
2.	corazón	A
3.	máquina	E
4.	carácter	G
5.	mención	A
6.	Núñez	G
7.	tiendas	G
8.	calcetín	A
9.	gramática	E
10.	venderás	A
11.	ciudad	A
12.	suéter	G
13.	dificultad	A
14.	Múzquiz	G
15.	médicos	E
16.	pasión	A
17.	hermosa	G
18.	Pacífico	E
19.	fútbol	G
20.	capitán	A

Page 103

1. La lección de francés no es difícil.
2. Ojalá que mi papá hable con el señor Vásquez
3. Los jóvenes también vienen por avión.
4. Los mecánicos trabajan en esta región.
5. El músico toca mi canción favorita.
6. Los demócratas se juntan aquí en esta mansión.
7. Verónica trabaja con Jesús todos los miércoles.
8. El líder de la nación es Héctor Galván.
9. Ángel Juárez es presidente de la unión.
10. Nélida Ramírez tiene una pensión.

Page 105

Mi hermano Adrián dice que Verónica le dijo que la lección de inglés no es difícil. En esta región, todas las escuelas también enseñan francés. Todos dicen que los exámenes son fáciles.

René Chávez trabajó con la unión local número 654. Ganaba mil dólares por semana. Ahora recibe una pensión muy buena. Con ese dinero compró una mansión muy grande. Allí vive muy feliz.

Page 106

1. huésped — G
2. libertad — A
3. plátano — E
4. Guzmán — A
5. Martínez — G
6. escribí — A
7. república — E
8. padres — G
9. azúcar — G
10. canción — A
11. Suárez — G
12. pájaro — E
13. pizarra — G
14. además — A
15. salud — A
16. hispánico — E
17. compraré — A
18. automóvil — G
19. nación — A
20. Francisco — G

Page 107

1. o pi **nión**
2. di rec **ción**
3. po bla **ción**
4. e lec **ción**
5. con fe **sión**
6. con di **ción**
7. ex pli ca **ción**
8. ge ne ra **ción**
9. con tes ta **ción**
10. com pa ra **ción**
11. de ses pe ra **ción**
12. ad mi nis tra **ción**

Page 108

1. Con cep **ción**.
2. A sun **ción**
3. En car na **ción**.
4. Ca **rrión**   V

1. Cons ti tu **ción**
2. Mi gra **ción**
3. Go ber na **ción**
4. Su per vi **sión**
5. Ad mi nis tra **ción**
6. Ins pec **ción**

P 109 & P 111 on the next Answer Sheet

Page 110

1. José López tiene mi contestación.
2. El papá de Jesús trabaja con la administración.
3. La clase de Francés no tiene supervisión.
4. El líder de los demócratas es Andrés Carrión.
5. La Migración vino por Héctor Fernández.
6. El profesor Vélez tiene mi explicación.
7. Encarnación trabajó en el Departamento de Inspección.
8. Agustín Rodríguez es un católico bueno.
9. Los exámenes de la clase de religión son fáciles.
10. Víctor compró una televisión nueva.

Page 112

El señor Carrión y su esposa Carmen viven en el cuarto número 5. La condición del hotel no es buena. Tiene en sofá café chico. También tiene una televisión con el color débil. Ellos vivirán allí un año.

Nicolás Martínez recibió una carta de su prima Nélida con cien dólares. Con ese dinero llevó a su novia Concepción a comer a un restaurante. Después le compró un perfume y una loción muy buena.

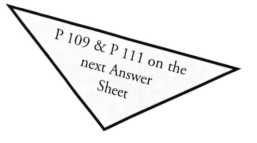

Page 109

1. fáciles
2. débil
3. unión
4. miércoles
5. universidad
6. perros
7. comparación
8. reloj
9. demócrata
10. ángel
11. Calderón
12. señor
13. almacén
14. elección
15. árbol
16. teléfonos
17. televisor
18. autobús
19. población
20. Meléndrez

Page 111

1. general   A
2. confesión   A
3. difícil   G
4. Mónica   E
5. secretaria   A
6. alemán   G
7. histórico   E
8. cáncer   G
9. comerás   A
10. joven   G
11. lápices   E
12. algodón   A
13. población   A
14. automático   E
15. cárcel   G
16. sábado   E
17. huésped   G
18. Marisol   A
19. acción   A
20. calles   G

Page 113

1. suéter   G
2. Cásares   E
3. universidad   A
4. adiós   A
5. desesperación   A
6. televisor   A
7. pájaro   E
8. Antonio   G
9. ángel   G
10. alemán   A
11. lecciones   G
12. hablaré   A
13. simpático   E
14. González   G
15. inspección   A
16. familia   E
17. república   G
18. difícil   A
19. misión   G
20. cáncer   G

Page 115

1. **mí** o
2. pa **ís**
3. **tí** a
4. **rí** o
5. ra **íz**
6. **mí** a
7. ma **íz**
8. **dí** a
9. **frí** o
10. co **mí** a
11. vi **ví** a
12. co **rrí** a

Page 116

1. **Dí** az
2. **Rí** os
3. Ra **úl**
4. A **í** da
5. Lu **cí** a
6. E **lí** as
7. Sa **úl**
8. Ma **rí** a
9. So **fí** a
10. Ro **cí** o

Page 118 is on the next Answer Sheet

Page 117

1. canción
2. Ángeles
3. ciudad
4. automóvil
5. comía
6. secretaria
7. jardín
8. Castillón
9. amistad
10. bailarín
11. médico
12. Aída
13. reloj
14. explicación
15. muchos
16. lápiz
17. maíz
18. también
19. población
20. venderás

Page 119

1. inútil   G
2. después   A
3. teléfono   E
4. corazón   A
5. Aguilar   A
6. míos   G
7. calcetín   A
8. sábado   E
9. Domínguez   G
10. administrador   A
11. autobús   A
12. mexicano   G
13. demócrata   E
14. ojalá   A
15. Raquel   A
16. árbol   G
17. Velásquez   G
18. música   E
19. amigo   G
20. Nicolás   A

Page 118

1. Mi tío César juega béisbol aquí.
2. El capitán Córdova vivia en México.
3. Raúl corría en el parque el miércoles.
4. Yo compraré un violín el día ocho.
5. Los jóvenes escriben la lección fácil.
6. Tomás compró la televisión por cien dólares.
7. Mi tía Verónica vendió su avión nuevo.
8. María trabajó allí en ese almacén.
9. Saúl tenía la máquina mía.
10. Este país tiene un río muy frío.

Page 120

Los jóvenes estudiaban la lección de inglés en la casa de mi tío José. Era muy fácil porque el libro tenía la explicación completa. Ellos quieren estudiar mucho porque los exámenes son el dia veinte.

Mi tío Rubén Escobar trabajó en esta ciudad. Todos los días viajaba por autobús. Comía en un café cerca del río. Los sábados y domingos no trabajaba porque se iba a ver los juegos de béisbol.

Page 121

1. fútbol — G
2. Sofía — G
3. sílaba — E
4. comerás — A
5. inteligente — G
6. política — E
7. tenía — G
8. también — A
9. Gabriel — A
10. lápices — E
11. contestación — A
12. periódico — E
13. violín — A
14. chocolates — G
15. matiné — A
16. fáciles — E
17. mención — A
18. lápiz — G
19. canciones — G
20. Obregón — A

Page 122

1. po li cí a
2. li bre rí a
3. lo te rí a
4. mi no rí a
5. fru te rí a
6. com pa ñí a
7. es cri bí a
8. to da ví a
9. e co no mí a
10. ca fe te rí a
11. fi lo so fí a
12. za pa te rí a

Page 123

1. de **bí** a
2. sa **lí** a
3. ven **dí** a
4. a sis **tí** a
5. le **í** a
6. ve **í** a
7. re **í** a
8. a pren de **rí** a
9. ha bla **rí** a
10. re ci **bí** a
11. da **rí** a mos
12. vol ve **rí** an

Page 124

1. Gar **cí** a
2. Me **jí** a
3. To **bí** as
4. Fa **rí** as
5. Ma **cí** as
6. Ma **tí** as
7. E fra **ín**
8. E lo **í** sa
9. Ro sa **lí** a
10. Cha va **rrí** a
11. Ren te **rí** a
12. Za ca **rí** as
13. Es con **trí** as
14. E che ve **rrí** a
15. I sa **í** as

Page 125

1. azúcar
2. librería
3. religión
4. calculador
5. dólares
6. familia
7. japonés
8. líder
9. felicidad
10. compañía
11. Vásquez
12. ferrocarril
13. zapatería
14. automático
15. Alarcón
16. papeles

Page 127

1. gramática — E
2. hermanos — G
3. lotería — G
4. ayer — A
5. plátanos — E
6. capital — A
7. carácter — G
8. recibí — A
9. reía — G
10. Encarnación — A
11. zapato — G
12. números — E
13. Gómez — G
14. automóvil — G
15. Chavarría — G
16. supervisión — A
17. hablaría — G
18. señoritas — G
19. católico — E
20. raíz — A

Page 129

1. japonés — A
2. fáciles — E
3. Eduardo — G
4. huésped — G
5. reloj — A
6. Atlántico — E
7. inútil — G
8. central — A
9. zapatos — G
10. demócrata — E
11. Sofía — G
12. ojalá — A
13. americano — G
14. abrirá — A
15. cadáver — G
16. mujer — A
17. Leticia — G
18. dólares — E
19. débil — G
20. frutería — G

Page 126

1. La economía de México es muy débil.
2. Ramón veía a María todos los días.
3. Mi tía Josefina vendía la máquina de escribir.
4. La mamá de Raúl leía el periódico.
5. El capitán Juárez era el líder de los policías.
6. La señora Martínez todavía no recibía los lápices.
7. César siempre corría después de Matías.
8. Este país tenía muchas compañías de azúcar.
9. Eloísa salía del almacén con Cristóbal.
10. Mi tío Tomás vivirá en mí casa.

Page 128

Víctor Macías estudia la lección de matemáticas. Los problemas no son fáciles. Mañana hablará con el profesor Hernández y después irá a la librería. El miércoles y el jueves serán los exámenes.

Mi tío Héctor leía el periódico todos los días. Allí veía los números de la lotería. El año pasado, recibió un millón de dólares. Después compró una cafetería y vende comida mexicana.

Page 132

1. cárcel
2. política
3. presidente
4. autobús
5. sí
6. Patricia
7. minoría
8. mi
9. mención
10. difícil
11. tenía
12. adiós
13. sé
14. simpático
15. pizarras
16. jardín
17. estéril
18. joven
19. éste
20. investigador

Page 134

1. estudiaré   A
2. García   G
3. él   A
4. sábado   E
5. vendió   A
6. dineros   G
7. doctor   A
8. tu   A
9. difícil   G
10. demócrata   E
11. aquel   A
12. Javier   A
13. fácil   G
14. sí   A
15. periódico   E
16. feliz   A
17. autobús   A
18. árbol   G
19. mí   A
20. plátano   E

Page 136

1. escribí   A
2. tú   A   pron.
3. reloj   A
4. fútbol   G
5. hispánico   E
6. Chacón   A
7. fácil   G
8. dé   A   verb
9. calcetín   A
10. padres   G
11. máquina   E
12. Sánchez   G
13. nariz   A
14. ojalá   A
15. éste   G   pron.
16. sábado   E
17. profesión   A
18. filosofía   G
19. joven   G
20. Sí   A   adv.

Page 133

1. Tú y tu tío Ramón vivirán con él.
2. Este violín lo compró mi papá para mí.
3. Después él vivió aquí.
4. Sí, el líder hablará con Joaquín Gómez.
5. Mi mamá compró mucho té en el almacén.
6. El japonés comió más que Mónica.
7. El capitán dijo que éste es mío.
8. Los jóvenes comprarán aquél.
9. Tú y él venderán tu sofá.
10. El señor Pérez quiere que yo dé un millón dé dólares.

Page 135

El profesor Cásares dijo que antes él corría en el parque. Todos los días salía en las tardes a correr. Ayer compró un suéter para mí. Quiere que yo corra con él en las noches. Yo no sé si podré.

Mi papá vivió en México hace cuatro años. Dice que él tenía una zapatería. Allí trabajaba tu tío Cándido Fernández también. Ellos vivían en un hotel cerca de una cafetería.

Page 138
1. ¿Cómo?
2. ¿Cuál?
3. ¿Quién?
4. ¿Dónde?
5. ¿Cuánto?
6. ¿Cuándo?
7. ¿Cuáles?
8. ¿Cuántos?
9. ¿Ése?
10. ¿Éste?

Page 139
1. ¡Cómo!
2. ¡Cuál!
3. ¡Quién!
4. ¡Dónde!
5. ¡Cuánto!
6. ¡Cuándo!
7. ¡Cuáles!
8. ¡Cuántos!
9. ¡Ése!
10. ¡Éste!

Page 140
1. vendió
2. débil
3. gramática
4. explicación
5. sólo
6. ¿Cuánto?
7. maíz
8. automóvil
9. ciudad
10. Atlántico
11. autobús
12. secretaria
13. de
14. ¡Quién!
15. ferrocarril
16. recibí
17. reía
18. comparación
19. ¿Dónde?
20. cuando

Page 142
1. después A
2. vivía G
3. ¿Qué? A
4. exámenes E
5. televisión A
6. cáncer G
7. sé A
8. tenía G
9. algodón A
10. jóvenes E
11. inglés A
12. ¡Cuándo! G
13. elección A
14. tu A
15. ¿Quién? A
16. Juárez G
17. demócrata E
18. aquí A
19. inútil G
20. azul A

Page 141
1. ¿Dónde compró este violín tu papá?
2. ¡Cuánto trabajó Víctor Solís!
3. Tu tío comerá en la cafetería con Sofía.
4. ¿El señor Martínez vivía con él?
5. ¡Qué tenía tu tía María!
6. Tú venderás la televisión por mí.
7. Yo sé que tú tienes cinco dólares.
8. Yo estudiaré el inglés todos los días.
9. ¡Cómo vivió Elías aquí!
10. ¿Quién leía el periódico de Benjamín Méndez?

Page 143
¿Qué tenía tu tía anoche? Héctor dijo que ella hablaba de la política con el capitán Juárez. También dijo que ella es policía y que trabajaba en la cárcel. ¿Cuándo irás a hablar con ella?

¿Dónde viven tus tíos? Verónica me dice que antes ellos vivían en América. Ahora viven en México. Allí él tiene un trabajo muy fácil en una compañía grande. ¿Cuánto dinero recibirá?

Page 144

1. ciudad — A
2. hispánico — E
3. mi — A (adj)
4. útil — G
5. todavía — G
6. leche — G
7. condición — A
8. huésped — G
9. sí — A (adv)
10. fácil — G
11. comerás — A
12. azúcar — G
13. feliz — A
14. Elías — G
15. ¿Dónde? — G
16. dólares — E
17. después — A
18. difícil — G
19. plátano — E
20. ¡Cuáles! — G

Page 145

1. Carácter — G
2. mayoría — G
3. el libro — A (art)
4. asistía — G
5. autobús — A
6. director — A
7. jardín — A
8. cárcel — G
9. para mí — A (pro)
10. Márquez — G
11. religión — A
12. difícil — G
13. padre — G
14. muchos — G
15. ¿Cuándo? — G
16. central — A
17. número — E
18. recibía — G
19. fácil — G
20. sábado — E

Page 147

1. **tó** ma lo
2. **cóm** pra los
3. **cór** ta la
4. **fír** ma los
5. es **tú** dia lo
6. es **crí** be me
7. **llé** va se lo
8. **có** me te lo
9. **cán** ta se la
10. **dí** ga me lo
11. **pí** de se lo
12. **á** bre se lo

Page 148

1. economía
2. líder
3. cuanto
4. aquél
5. escríbeme
6. venderás
7. apartamento
8. ángel
9. té
10. ojalá
11. dígamelo
12. exámenes
13. ¿ése?
14. corría
15. joven
16. carácter
17. sólo
18. estúdialo
19. fútbol
20. llévaselo

Page 151 is on the next Answer sheet

Page 149

1. Tú véndeselo a mi tío por cien dólares.
2. Háblame por teléfono el sábado.
3. Cómpralos para Tomas y para mí.
4. Nicolás y él son médicos en este hospital.
5. La lección de inglés es muy difícil.
6. Tú llévaselo al mecánico el miércoles.
7. En América hay muchos políticos demócratas.
8. Escríbeme la lección de matemáticas aquí.
9. ¿Cuándo son mis exámenes?
10. Tú pídeselo al profesor Cárdenas.

Page 150

Mi hermano Hipólito quiere que tú compres cinco lápices. Cómpralos en ese almacén. Después llévaselos a su cuarto. René quiere un lápiz también. Véndeselo por un dólar. ¿Cuándo los comprarás?

¿Quién vive en este apartamento? Me dicen que dos jóvenes. Se llaman Elías y José. Ellos pagan cien dólares de renta. Mañana se irán a Panamá. A mí me gusta aquí. Háblame por teléfono para verlos.

Accents - Answer Sheet

Spanish Accents

Page 151

1. supervisiön A
2. mayoría G
3. calcetín A
4. cántasela S
5. útil G
6. máquina E
7. plural A
8. Antonio G
9. débil G
10. cómetelo S
11. filosofía G
12. chocolate G
13. Dávila E
14. espanol A
15. córtala E
16. María G
17. aúcar G
18. pantalón A
19. dígamelo S
20. número E

Page 152

1. amistad A
2. ¿Dónde? G
3. dígamelo S
4. carretera G
5. exámenes E
6. escribía G
7. confesión A
8. llévaselo S
9. útil G
10. América E
11. violín A
12. tenía G
13. pídeselo S
14. Francisco G
15. saludaré A
16. corría G
17. háblame E
18. ¡Cuáles! G
19. véndeselo S
20. adiós A

Page 154

1. **fá** cil men te
2. **dé** bil men te
3. his **tó** ri ca men te
4. po **lí** ti ca men te
5. di **fí** cil men te
6. ma te **má** ti ca men te
7. **trá** gi ca men te
8. **ló** gi ca men te
9. e co **nó** mi ca men te
10. au to **má** ti ca men te

Page 155

1. ma **lí** si mo
2. a zu **lí** si mo
3. ro **jí** si ma
4. bue **ní** si mo
5. de bi **lí** si mo
6. her mo **sí** si ma
7. fuer **tí** si mo
8. gran **dí** si mos
9. ca **rí** si mo
10. ba ra **tí** si mas
11. mu **chí** si mo
12. di fi ci **lí** si mo

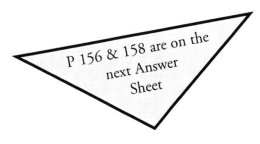

P 156 & 158 are on the next Answer Sheet

Page 157

1. Víctor Ramírez tiene el corazón debilísimo.
2. Antes tú corrías rápidamente.
3. Ojalá que este carro corra económicamente.
4. ¿Cuándo comprarás este sofá grandísimo?
5. Háblame por teléfono para ir a la librería.
6. Mi tío Andrés murió trágicamente.
7. René compró este autobús baratísimo.
8. José vendió su carro fácilmente.
9. Martín quiere a María muchísimo.
10. La puerta se abrió automáticamente.

Page 159

Verónica es una muchacha buenísima. Ayer yo comí con ella en un café. Allí me ayudó con la lección de matemáticas. Ella la aprendió fácilmente. Para mí es muy difícil porque yo no estudio mucho.

Mi tío César es el alcalde de la ciudad. Políticamente, él es un demócrata. Mi primo Tobías también es un político. Los dos dicen que la economía del país de Los Estados Unidos es fuertísima.

Page 156

1. además
2. tómalo
3. inteligente
4. fuertísimo
5. jóvenes
6. lógicamente
7. carácter
8. café
9. cómetelo
10. televisor
11. lápiz
12. leía
13. ¿Cuándo?
14. feliz
15. teléfono
16. buenísima
17. Méndez
18. compañía
19. políticamente
20. inglés

Page 158

1. María — G
2. ciudad — A
3. fírmalos — E
4. ¡Cómo! — G
5. fácilmente — S
6. estudiaré — A
7. población — A
8. fútbol — G
9. república — E
10. librería — G
11. comparación — A
12. rápidamente — S
13. muchísimo — E
14. luna — G
15. vivirán — A
16. difícilmente — S
17. inútil — G
18. Castillón — A
19. hermosísima — E
20. matemáticamente — S

Page 160

1. V
2. F
3. V
4. V
5. F
6. V
7. F
8. F
9. V
10. V
11. F
12. F
13. V
14. F
15. V
16. F
17. V
18. F
19. V
20. V

Page 161

1. estúdialo — E
2. ¿Cuáles? — G
3. Concepción — A
4. dígamelo — S
5. Javier — A
6. exámenes — E
7. facilísimo — E
8. niños — G
9. corazón — A
10. automática — E
11. débilmente — S
12. francés — A
13. árbol — G
14. cántasela — S
15. café — A
16. simpático — E
17. difícilmente — S
18. ¡Cómo! — G
19. Castillón — A
20. mecánico — E

Page 162

1. cómpralos — E
2. ¡Qué! — A
3. aprendería — G
4. fácilmente — S
5. Arturo — G
6. miércoles — E
7. muchísimo — E
8. televisión — A
9. después — A
10. pídeselo — S
11. lápices — E
12. joven — G
13. ¿Cuántos? — G
14. compramelas — S
15. azulísimo — E
16. dólares — E